do not have in Jan/A

NAZI HUNTER: Simon Wiesenthal

He is fairly tall, broad shouldered, has thick, dark hair, streaked with gray. In no way unusual looking, Simon Wiesenthal has had a life marked with incredible experiences and accomplishments, the greatest of which was undoubtedly his discovery of the trail that led to Adolf Eichmann in hiding. Wiesenthal was himself a concentration camp inmate under the Nazis and twice stood above his own grave awaiting imminent execution. Eluding death, he survived until the end of the war when he was stirred by the many accounts of the experiences of fellow ex-prisoners to begin tracing the now-dispersed SS members who had terrorized and slaughtered millions. This book tells of the courage and persistence of a man who does not shirk his obligation to help humanity remember its past.

OTHER BOOKS BY IRIS NOBLE

NAZI HUNTER

Simon Wiesenthal

By IRIS NOBLE

JULIAN MESSNER
NEW YORK

Manufactured in the United States of America

Design by Miriam Temple

Library of Congress Cataloging in Publication Data
Noble, Iris.
    Nazi hunter, Simon Wiesenthal.
    Includes index.
    SUMMARY: Presents an account of the activities
of Simon Wiesenthal who has been instrumental
in locating and prosecuting members of the Nazi
SS, many of whom disappeared at the end of
World War II.
    1. Wiesenthal Simon—Juvenile literature.
2. Holocaust, Jewish (1939-1945)—Juvenile
literature.   3. War criminals—Juvenile literature.
[1. Wiesenthal, Simon.   2. War criminals—
Germany.   3. Holocaust, Jewish (1939-1945)]
I. Title.
D810.J4N55   364.12′092′4 [B] [92]   79-15783
ISBN 0-671-32964-2

ACKNOWLEDGMENT

The author wishes to thank Simon Wiesenthal and Opera Mundi, Paris, for permission to use as source material Mr. Wiesenthal's book, *The Murderers Among Us.*

Introduction

On a warm, sunshiny day in 1961, a man walked through
the streets of Jerusalem. Ordinarily he would have been
alert to all the sights and sounds around him: the house-
wives with shopping bags, schoolboys with books under their
arms or in satchels, the young girl traffic officers in their
uniforms, the shopkeepers, the taxis, and the tourist buses.

Today he was only half-aware of them. His stride had
purpose. Broad-shouldered and fairly tall—five foot eleven
inches—he pushed his way easily through the crowds. There
was nothing particularly arresting about his face, which
seemed long because his thick, dark hair, streaked with
gray, was beginning to recede and give him a high forehead.
His small mustache was like that worn by many businessmen
in Jerusalem.

Yet now and then, someone stopped to look at him. Here
and there a couple whispered about him as he passed.
From a coffee shop he heard his name spoken softly and in
awe: "It's Wiesenthal!"

Simon Wiesenthal went on, unheeding, until he reached
the large, grim building where the trial was being held.
Ringing it outside were Israeli soldiers with submachine

7

guns. A policewoman in a sentry box examined his ticket and apologized for having to search him for any gun, tape recorder or camera he might be carrying. It had to be done. This was no ordinary trial.

He passed in and took his privileged seat in the gallery. From there he could look down upon the public seats and across them to the high podium, and as he watched a door opened and the three robed judges filed in to take their places on that podium. There was a general stir. Everyone rose. Now Simon Wiesenthal could distinguish the two counsels in their black gowns, the one for the defense and the other for the prosecution.

What riveted everyone's eyes now was the bulletproof large glass box. A sound—half-anguish, half-anger—swept over the courtroom as the prisoner emerged from another door and, accompanied by guards, walked to that box and stood inside it.

"Your name?" the prisoner was asked.

"Adolf Eichmann," he answered.

If Simon Wiesenthal's attention was wholly on the prisoner, it is more than possible that Adolf Eichmann, as the routine preliminaries of the trial got underway, was very sure that Simon Wiesenthal was somewhere in the audience. Neither man had ever seen the other before yet they were bound together by a chain of hatred.

More than any other single person, Simon Wiesenthal was responsible for the pursuit, the capture, and the trial of Adolf Eichmann. Others had made the actual capture, just as others would prosecute now, but Wiesenthal had made it all possible.

In the Jerusalem courtroom Simon Wiesenthal saw Eichmann for the first time, yet he knew the man inside and out. He knew him from his childhood to the crowning triumphs of his evil career. He knew Eichmann's life as a fugitive and had followed him through all his hiding places, to his capture. He knew he would now see Eichmann confront the punishment he so richly deserved, as the man who had planned the deaths of so many millions of people. Eichmann had been the SS Gestapo head of the Nazi Bureau IV, which had organized the building of the concentration camps, had planned the way they would function, decided which gas chambers and burning ovens were most efficient, and handled all the transportation of the victims to those camps.

Eichmann was guilty of no single atrocity. He had never whipped, tortured, or killed a single Jew with his own hands. The inmates of the concentration camps did not even know his name until after the war was over.

Yet Simon Wiesenthal loathed this man far more than if he had been a dull-witted brute with a whip or gun in his hand. Eichmann had planned the murder of more than six million people methodically, carefully, and cold-bloodedly. Those who died were items in his ledgers. At the end of a good day he could enter the many thousands who had been gassed or shot or burned to death. The end of a bad day for him would be one in which transport had delayed sending the proper quota of victims to their death.

Responsible for the extermination of Jews, Eichmann had added gypsies to his concentration camp victims. In the prosecutor's hands was a telegram Simon Wiesenthal had found and turned over to him. It read: "Regarding transport of gypsies be informed that on Friday, 20.10.39, the first transport of Jews will depart Vienna. To this . . . 3–4 cars of gypsies are to be attached. . . . Because these transports must follow a schedule, a smooth execution of this matter is expected. (Signed) Eichmann."

"A smooth execution"—it did not mean anything to Eichmann that these were people. His ledgers must balance.

"Let me tell you something," Eichmann had once said, "Jewish death lists are my favorite reading matter before I go to sleep."

The prisoner Eichmann must often have cursed Wiesenthal—baffled as to why this Wiesenthal had pursued him so relentlessly. Of course, he was a Jew. He had been in concentration camps. But other Jews only wanted to forget. Those who had survived the camps had moved to Palestine or other countries. They wanted to put the Nazi years behind them.

What had turned Simon Wisenthal into a man dedicated to one purpose: bringing men like Eichmann and others to justice?

What, indeed. Simon Wiesenthal has become one of the world's greatest detectives, but he is also one of the strangest.

He has had no training in this work; he trained himself. He has no employer. He is now responsible to no police force, no government agency, and no private agency. He works in a shabby office and from voluntary contributions pays himself just enough to support his family. His assistants work for small salaries or for nothing because they believe in what he is doing.

Yet he is feared by men all over the world. Some are rich and powerful. They have found sanctuary in countries that will not deport Nazi criminals, but they are not free. As long as Simon Wiesenthal lives, they must stay where they are or risk a trial like Eichmann's. He has been responsible for the arrest of nearly a thousand former SS men.

The SS (the Schutzstaffel) was an elite corps, the special killers of the Nazi government during World War II. They were responsible only to their own leaders and then to Heinrich Himmler and Adolf Hitler. They were feared as much by army generals as they were by ordinary Germans.

They were the murderers of millions of people. They are the men Simon hunts.

When Simon Wiesenthal walked out of the courtroom that first day of the Eichmann trial, he felt as if he were coming out of darkness into light. Many of the people he passed must have been survivors of concentration camps. Now they were rebuilding their lives. Many of them could work again; love and laugh again, in spite of the scars they bore and the loved ones left behind in the mass graves of the death camps.

He felt certain that Eichmann would pay the death penalty. Perhaps some of the people in Jerusalem would look upon it as revenge for what they had suffered. Simon Wiesenthal no longer felt that way.

He had wanted Eichmann brought to trial so that the past would not be forgotten. The world was beginning to forget. This trial would jolt memories. That terrible holocaust of death *must not* be forgotten, or it might happen again. Wiesenthal's pursuit was of men, but it was the evil ideas of these men he wanted to destroy.

It had not always been so. In the beginning he, too, had wanted revenge—pure, simple, personal, furious revenge.

Chapter One

Simon Wiesenthal was born in 1908 in Buczacs in the area called Galicia. It was a beautiful part of eastern Europe but a troubled part, constantly fought over by Austria, Poland, and the Russian Ukranians.

When Simon was born Galicia was still part of the Austro-Hungarian Empire. In the first World War Austria and Germany were allies, and Simon's father left his wholesale business to fight. Another Austrian also fought in that war and became a corporal. His name was Adolf Hitler.

In later years Hitler built much of his anti-Semitic propaganda on the claim that all Jews had stayed home and gotten rich during that war, while honest Germans fought and died. Yet Hitler lived through the war while Simon's father was killed in battle. Mr. Wiesenthal was a Jew.

Of the nine thousand people in Buczacs, six thousand were Jewish. They were a majority in the town because they were forbidden to own farmland. The Galician Poles and Ukranians despised the landless Jews, but it was a contempt mixed with envy. With the growth of trade and industry some Jews became prosperous. However, most Jews were poor tradesmen or craftsmen, tailors, shoemakers.

Still, the envy was there. Periodically it erupted into a pogrom, a brutal attack upon the Jews. Or else there would be a border war and the victors and defeated both took out their savage emotions upon these people. There would be another pogrom.

In 1920, when Simon was twelve, there was a Polish-Russian war. The Russian-Ukranian Cossacks rode into Buczacs. Temporarily victorious, they made for the taverns and wine shops. Drunk, they roamed the streets looking for shops to loot and for Jews to beat up.

Like all the Jewish families, the Wiesenthals barricaded the door of their house. They stayed indoors and listened fearfully to the wild shouts, the drunken laughter, the furious racing of the Cossack horses—and now and then a scream.

Simon's mother was running out of food. The situation became desperate. A chance must be taken. When the street in front of their house seemed momentarily quiet, she sent Simon running across the street to borrow yeast from a neighbor so she could make bread.

Simon was halfway across when a mounted Ukranian came pounding around the corner. The Cossack charged at the boy, leaned out of his saddle and swiped at Simon with his saber. He rode on, laughing, and leaving Simon with a thigh so badly slashed that the neighbors had to dash out and carry the bleeding boy inside.

The wound healed but he would carry that scar on his thigh all his life.

The Ukranians were defeated, and Galicia became a part of Poland. For many years after that there was peace for the Wiesenthals. Many Poles were anti-Semitic, but they showed it usually in discrimination, not violence.

In 1925 Mrs. Wiesenthal remarried, and the family moved to Dolina in the Carpathian Mountains, where Simon's new stepfather owned a tile factory. Simon loved Dolina. The setting was beautiful. He could hike and ride horseback along the mountain trails. It was, however, only a vacation spot for him because he was ready for college. He wanted to enter the Technical Institute of Lwow, the nearest big city in Poland, but he was rejected. The small quota for Jewish students was already filled. Instead, he went to Prague, Czechoslovakia, and entered the Czech Technical Institute. His field was architecture.

He was quick-witted and intelligent. His fellow students saw in him a good-looking, slim young man, experimenting with a neat, dark mustache, carrying his height with a proud air. That pride and the direct way in which he looked at everyone might have caused him trouble with the Christian Czechs in college, but Simon also had a sense of humor and a lot of small jokes. He was, therefore, popular with Czechs and Jews alike.

After graduation he went to Lwow in Poland and began his architectural practice. He specialized in the design of fine homes rather than office or factory buildings. By 1936 he had grown so successful he could afford to marry Cyla Muller, his very pretty, blonde sweetheart from their high school days.

The next few years were happy ones for the Wiesenthals, but they were aware of and disturbed by what was going on in Germany. They thought the events taking place there would not affect their lives, but they worried for the German Jews.

In 1933 Adolf Hitler had been proclaimed Chancellor of Germany. Immediately he had "suspended" the civil rights of the constitution, and imposed the death penalty for "crimes against the public security." Joseph Goebbels was appointed Minister for People's Enlightenment and Propaganda, and the Jew-hating Goebbels instituted book-burnings. Onto these bonfires went every book contrary to Hitler's and Goebbels's ideas.

Heinrich Himmler was given full police power to destroy any opposition to Hitler by terror methods. The SS and Gestapo came into being. Communists, Socialists, priests, and educators who spoke against Hitler were swept into prisons. On April 1 a nationwide boycott against Jewish doctors, lawyers, and business houses was officially ordered.

In 1934 Hitler declared himself sole head of the German state, with the total power of a dictator.

And in 1935 came the infamous "Nuremberg Laws" which took away all rights of citizenship from Jews. They must register as Jews; they could not marry Gentiles; Jewish students were turned out of schools and universities.

The Wiesenthals were shocked. Anti-Semitism was expected in Poland, but Germany had long been a civilized nation. German Jews had always been a strong thread in the fabric of German life. They had contributed so much to German business and to German culture. A great many of the nation's most famous artists, writers, musicians, teachers, playwrights, and philosophers had been Jews.

Discussing this with their friends, Simon and Cyla found all sorts of opinions. Some held that Hitler was a madman; he'd soon be put in an asylum. Others felt that France and England would not permit him to go on building up his army and air force: they would step in and crush him. Still others shrugged: Jews had suffered before, all through history, and now the German Jews must face a temporary unpleasantness. It would pass.

In 1936 Hitler marched his troops into the Rhineland, the demilitarized zone between France and Germany, and France did nothing but protest.

Encouraged by France's weakness, Hitler summoned the Austrian Chancellor to Berchtesgaden on February 12, 1938, and presented him with an ultimatum: stop interfering with the Austrian Nazi Party or Germany would march in and take over. On March 12 there was a new Austrian Chancellor named Seyss-Inquart, a tool of Hitler's, and the Anschluss was announced. The Anschluss was the official act which incorporated Austria into the German Reich, or empire.

German troops did march into Austria, but they were met by cheering crowds. The jackboots of the uniformed Austrian Nazis joined with those of the German troops, stamping in unison along the streets, as Austrians chanted: "Austria—awake! Judah—perish!"

Judah meant the Jews. Now the Nuremberg Laws reached into Austria. Austrian Jews suffered as badly as did German Jews when, on November 9 and 10, came the "Crystal Night." Led by the SS men, soldiers and civilians alike went on a terrible rampage of smashing Jewish stores and businesses and homes, and burning synagogues. The name for the night came from the shattered glass that littered the sidewalks in front of stores and shops.

Homes were entered, Jews were pushed out into the streets, beaten, and forced to crawl on bloody knees among the sharp splinters of glass. "Crystal Night" was far too pretty a name for such nights of horror.

Hitler now set his sights on Czechoslovakia, claiming that the minority Germans in that nation were not treated fairly. It was a lie, but Hitler was the master of the Big Lie.

Worried that Hitler's aggression might continue and spread farther in Europe, the Prime Minister of England flew to Germany and met with Hitler, Mussolini, dictator of Italy, and the Premier of France. Out of this meeting came the shameful Munich Pact. The British and French agreed to let Hitler have his way in Czechoslovakia in return for his promise that this would be the last demand he would make. He promised he wanted no more territory.

Like everyone else, Simon Wiesenthal hoped this was true. If it was a lie, then Poland would surely be Hitler's next victim.

Some Jews were able to leave Poland, but most could not. It was not an easy matter to get a visa so they could go to live in another country. The British were restricting immigration to Palestine. America and other nations had quotas for immigration, and there were more applicants for visas to America than the quotas allowed.

Besides, people like the Wiesenthals had strong roots in Poland and ties to their families, friends, and work. They felt they could survive persecution. They might be forced to live in restricted Jewish ghettos as they had in the past. If so, they could do this until the anti-Semitic madness passed.

No one could imagine that what they faced was not just persecution, but mass death.

On August 23 the Soviet Union and Germany signed a non-aggression pact. This was a blow. Now Hitler did not need to fear a strong enemy to the east or opposition to his plans for Poland.

In all fairness, the Soviet Union had approached France and England—on March 17, 1938 and on March 20, 1939—with a plan to unite and stop Hitler before he went any further. But since the plan meant the Red Army would have to march through Poland to attack Hitler, Poland refused and England backed Poland. The Soviet Union made its own deal with Hitler then.

On September 1, 1939, Hitler's troops invaded Poland. England and France declared war, but they were unprepared, and in that same month Hitler conquered the western and middle part of Poland while Russia moved into the eastern part.

Lwow, where Simon Wiesenthal lived, was in the Soviet

zone. For peasants and factory workers the Soviet rule was pleasant, but merchants, manufacturers, and professional men were under suspicion of being enemies of Communism. Simon's stepfather was arrested and taken away. Simon had seen the danger, closed his architectural office and taken a job as a mechanic in a bedspring factory. By doing so he was able to keep his wife and mother safe.

Rumors began to reach Lwow that terrible things were happening to the Jews in German-held Poland, but no one could be certain. The Wiesenthals did not have to wait long to find out.

In 1940 Germany defeated the French and British armies in Europe and conquered Norway, Denmark, the Netherlands, Belgium, and France. Then, swollen with arrogance and vanity, Hitler broke his pact with the Soviet Union and, in 1941, invaded Russia.

Lwow fell quickly to the Germans. On the thirtieth of June the Wiesenthals saw the German uniforms in their city and, along with the regular troops, the dreaded SS killing squads.

Six thousand Jews were killed in the city within a few days.

Both his wife and mother stayed quietly in the Wiesenthal apartment, but Simon and a friend were hiding in the basement when they were arrested and taken off to Brigidki prison. In the courtyard of the prison they found about forty other Jews, all of them doctors or lawyers, teachers or engineers or architects. It seemed as if this were a special roundup of Jewish intellectuals.

They were ordered to face the prison wall and put their hands behind their backs. Next to each man was a wooden crate—his coffin.

A Ukranian policeman (Wiesenthal was to find that many Ukranian policemen joined the German SS and tried to prove they could be even more brutal) started at one end of the wall and began shooting each prisoner in the back of the neck. In between shots, while the body was thrown into the crate, the Ukranian drank vodka and ate sausage. Then he aimed his pistol at the next man and fired. Shots and dying cries and the hoarse, drunken shouts of the Ukranian filled Wiesenthal's ears, but, like all the rest, he was in a state of shock. It would soon be his turn. There was nothing he could do to prevent it. If he turned and ran there were other guards all over the place. He would not get more than a few steps before he was shot down.

Suddenly there was the familiar sound of the evening church bells. A guard called out that that was enough for one day; it was time to eat and drink.

Twenty Jews were left alive. They were taken to two large cells. Simon Wiesenthal was so stunned by the horror of what had taken place that he lay in the cell in a stupor until he heard someone come in and then a flashlight was turned full upon his face and he heard a voice saying, "Mr. Wiesenthal, what are *you* doing here?"

It was another policeman, an auxiliary. Simon recognized the voice. It was a Pole named Bodnar who had once been a construction foreman on houses which Simon had designed. They had liked and respected each other.

Bodner whispered that he could get Wiesenthal out of this death trap but it would not be easy. He would have to claim that Wiesenthal was a Russian spy and must be taken to the proper authorities to be questioned. Undoubtedly, Wiesenthal would get rough treatment but he could escape. Could Bodnar also rescue Mr. Gross, the friend with whom he had been arrested? Simon asked.

Bodnar agreed. His plan was a desperate one. He went to the prison authorities and accused Wiesenthal and Gross as Russian spies. They must go with him. The prison guards reluctantly agreed, but first they brought the two Jews in and beat them unmercifully. Simon Wiesenthal took the pain and the humiliation without complaint, knowing that Bodnar was looking on and ·suffering for him, but also knowing this was the only way his life could be spared.

Once Bodnar and Wiesenthal and Gross were out of the prison, the Pole turned his back and let the two men "escape."

Simon went home. It seemed as safe a place as any.

A few weeks later the decree came that all Jews must move into what had been the old Jewish ghetto of the city. Simon and Cyla Wiesenthal were only there for a few months before they were both moved to a concentration camp, but Simon's mother was left behind in the ghetto.

After a few months both husband and wife were moved again to a forced-labor camp of the Eastern Railroad Repair Works.

They did not understand all these moves, then. They could not know that Adolf Eichmann had begun his smooth, orderly operation of sending the unfit and elderly to death while the younger and stronger went to slave-labor camps to be worked to death. The elderly, the children, and pregnant women were told they would be taken east, for resettlement in conquered territory.

Many accepted this lie because to believe they were going to be sent to a terrible and certain death was more than decent people could imagine.

At the railroad repair yards, Simon Wiesenthal encountered the second miracle which was to help him survive. Most German bosses of such places, which used both free and slave labor, worked the slaves to exhaustion and fed them as little as possible. The Wiesenthals, however, found themselves working for a man named Guenthert, the exceptional German who hated what he was forced to do, and who ordered his German guards to behave correctly towards both the free Polish labor and the Jewish slaves.

Cyla Wiesenthal worked on the locomotives, polishing brass and nickel. Simon became a sign painter, drawing German swastika-and-eagle shields on captured Russian locomotives. He was working outside in the bitter winter weather one day when the boss came by and noticed his hands were blue with cold. Guenthert got into conversation with him and found that Simon had been an architect. From that time on, Simon Wiesenthal worked inside as a technician and draftsman.

The working hours were long; the food was the barest minimum to keep slave bodies alive, yet he and Cyla were surviving. He heard that conditions in the Lwow ghetto, where his mother lived, were not too bad, either.

Then came 1942. SS Gestapo Chief Reinhard Heydrich called the Wannsee conference, acting under orders from Hitler and Himmler, to decide on "The Final Solution of the Jewish Question." Adolf Eichmann was present. The final solution, it was agreed, should be the *total* extermination of all Jews.

Simon Wiesenthal knew nothing, then, of the conference or the "final solution;" he did not even know the name of Eichmann. But he saw the results. At the railroad yards he had a front-row view of the tragedies being enacted. He saw trainload after trainload full of wretched, bewildered, starving Jews being carried off to some unknown destination.

Simon did not dare ask where the trainloads were going. He knew the guards had a special hatred of him because he still held himself straight and tall, and went about his work as if were not afraid of them. They would have used any excuse to kill him. Only Guenthert's favor had protected him so far. But he heard someone else ask about the trains.

A guard laughed. "They're going to be resettled," he answered jeeringly.

Then Simon guessed. The trainloads were going to death. The day came when he faced the worst, the unbelievable horror. Old women from the Lwow ghetto were brought to the railway yards and forced into freight cars by SS guards. The freight cars stood in the yard for three days waiting for a locomotive. They were three very hot days, and the old women were without water all that time. Simon could hear their pitiful wails. He dared not approach them. The freight cars were out of bounds, surrounded by guards with guns.

But, under pretense of working, he looked. He didn't want to; he was afraid of what he might find. His eyes searched their faces, as they stood packed in so tight none could sit and none could fall.

Then he saw her. His mother. She stood with the rest, one hand outstretched, pleading with the guards for a drink of water.

Simon was close to madness. For seconds his mind darted feverishly around—he could get water—he could make a dash for the freight car—he would pull her out of it. Then sanity returned. Could he add to his mother's agony? Would she have to watch the guards shoot her son and see him die at her feet across the railroad tracks, his blood spurting out upon the ground?

There was no way he could possibly reach her or help her or save her.

Then he saw the train was finally hitched up and it moved away. He never saw his mother again, but the image of her in that freight car was burned deep into his brain. *Someday,* he swore to himself, *someday They will pay for her and for all the others. I'll make Them pay.*

He made a desperate resolve that, somehow, he would at least save Cyla. By now he knew most of the Poles working at the railroad yards. He also knew that some were in the Polish underground, secretly working against the Germans. They had confided to him that they wanted to blow up the whole Lwow railroad junction.

As a technician and draftsman, he had been sent by his immediate supervisor, Inspector Kohlrautz, all over the yards at one or another on special jobs—always accompanied by a guard, of course. Simom Wiesenthal had a retentive memory. Using his skill as an engineer-architect, he made secret maps of the entire junction, showing all the places where the Poles could set explosive charges to the best advantage.

He took the maps to the Poles. He had a proposition: they could have those maps if they would help Cyla escape and get her a place to live among Poles. It would not be difficult. With her blonde hair and a new, Polish name she would not be identified as a Jew.

They agreed. Cyla was smuggled out into Lwow.

Her husband did not see her go, but one day a Pole whispered to him to go that night to a remote part of the slave-labor camp and stand as close as he could to the barbed wire which encircled the yard. Simon did so. In the darkness his wife came to him. She was on one side of the barbed wire and he on the other, but they could reach through and touch hands and whisper to each other for a moment. It was dangerous. She had to hurry away, and as she went he wondered if he would ever see her again.

Now it was time to worry about himself. He was only thirty-four years old and his work was not hard labor; nevertheless, there was no guarantee that his boss could keep him if the SS men came in to raid the repair shop for the "useless" ones to be sent to concentration camps.

Through his Polish connections he bought two pistols. Inspector Kohlrautz saw them in his desk, and said nothing.

Kohlrautz was as anti-Nazi a German as was the boss, and if Wiesenthal wanted to shoot it out with the SS so much the better.

It happened that Wiesenthal had no chance to use his guns. He was outside painting special posters around the repair works to celebrate the birthday of Adolf Hitler, April 20, 1943, when an SS man suddenly appeared, ordered Wiesenthal and two others to come with him. It happened so quickly Simon had no way of reaching his desk and his guns. Kohlrautz and Guenthert made a protest. It was ignored. That seemed all they could do; nobody could directly defy the SS.

The three Jews were taken to a concentration camp, along with other slave-labor Jews picked up here and there at random as they went through Lwow. This is what Simon had always feared: that purely by chance he would be selected for death. The SS man hadn't particularly wanted him. He had only wanted so many victims rounded up as a special death offering in honor of Hitler's birthday.

At the camp they were taken to the "hose." They all had heard of it. They knew what it meant. The "hose" was a narrow corridor between two barbed wire fences. No one had ever walked through that corridor and come back alive.

Two by two, with Simon Wiesenthal and another man near the end, they marched on down the "hose." It opened up onto a sandpit where naked, dead bodies lay. Simon and his group were not the first victims to be slain that day.

They were told to take off all their clothing and pile it neatly in a truck. Then they were lined up facing the sandpit. An SS officer raised his pistol, walked behind the line of men and casually shot them, one after another. They fell, crying out in shock and agony, into their own sandpit graves.

Simon could hear the shots getting closer and closer to

where he stood at the end of the line. He closed his eyes and waited for the explosive crack to come behind him, waited for the pain and then the nothingness of death.

There was a roaring in his ears and he knew it was the beat of his own blood, speeded up by fear. There seemed to be another sound, far away, very faint; he thought it was his own name being called. He knew that could not be.

Chapter Two

"Wie—sen—thal!"

The cry came from the corridor. Simon did not believe he was hearing it. It was some horrible trick of his imagination. But it came again: "Wie—sen—thal!"

He *was* being called. It was not his imagination. He called out that he was Wiesenthal. He was told to turn around. Another SS man, breathless, came the last yards of the "hose" and said that whichever one was Wiesenthal was to come with him. The SS man, the executioner, protested. He was supposed to shoot forty–four people and if they took one away, how was he going to answer to his superiors?

But the order had come from his superiors so there was nothing he could do but watch Wiesenthal being led away. It was unheard-of, an incredible thing! No Jew had ever before walked *back* through the "hose."

The truck was in the courtyard and Wiesenthal was ordered to get his clothes and put them on. Then he was taken back to the railroad repair shop where Inspector Kohlrautz assured the SS officer that it was a good thing Wiesenthal had been rescued in time. He was their best sign painter and it would have been very awkward for all of them if the Hitler posters were not finished in time for the great celebration that evening.

When the SS man left Kohlrautz looked at Wiesenthal and gave a great sigh of relief. Simon could hardly speak his gratitude. Condemned to death, he had been returned to life and could scarcely believe it. Kohlrautz had telephoned to the concentration camp commander and had insisted that Wiesenthal was too valuable to the repair works to be killed.

Why? Why did he and others take chances to perform the miracles which spared Simon Wiesenthal's life? Two other Jews had gone from the railroad yards into the "hose" and had not been called back. Why was a special effort made to save Wiesenthal?

Partly what Kohlrautz had told the commander was true: because of Wiesenthal's technical training and skill he was a valuable worker, but this was not the only reason. Then, as today, Simon Wiesenthal impressed people with his personality, with his intelligence, his dignity, his flashes of humor, and his sense of justice in what was due to himself and to others. Kohlrautz and Guenthert admired him.

But not even Kohlrautz could save him forever. In September of 1943 came the order that all Jewish slave labor working at the railway would have to sleep at the concentration camp and be marched under guard morning and night to and from work. When this happened Wiesenthal would be marked for death. The very qualities which made Kohlrautz and Guenthert respect him would irritate the SS bullies. A pistol shot would prove their power.

He saw it in their eyes as he walked, straight-backed, between them on his way from work to the concentration camp. He knew he had to escape.

Sitting at his desk on the morning of October 2, he waited for Kohlrautz to come by and then asked him for a pass into

Lwow to buy drafting supplies. Kohlrautz gave it to him without a word. The look that passed between them said it all—*goodbye—good luck—God be with you.*

While Wiesenthal deftly slid the two pistols into his pockets, Kohlrautz wrote out another pass for Arthur Scheiman, a friend of Simon's, and then went for the guard who was obliged to accompany prisoners into the city. He came back with the stupidest Ukranian he could find, a man who had just come to the district and did not know Lwow well.

It was simple for Wiesenthal and his friend to get rid of the policeman. They went to a stationery store which they knew had a back entrance, and they slipped out of it while the Ukranian had his attention on the goods in the store.

Both had friends in the city. They separated for a while. Scheiman went to his Ukranian wife while Wiesenthal sought refuge with a Polish family.

They were "free" for a little more than eight months, although it was scarcely freedom, being smuggled from one house to another, hiding in closets, and finally both living in the basement under the apartment of friends. The basement had a sand floor covered loosely with boards. They dug a trench just long and wide enough to hold them both, and whenever there was an alarm of a German search, they lay there and pulled over boards to cover themselves.

They were hunted men. They were no longer nameless Jews. They were *the* Wiesenthal and Schieman who had escaped. The arrogant honor of the SS demanded they be found. The Gestapo would never stop searching for them.

The great thing, for Simon, about those months of freedom was that he could catch up on all the news which German newspapers and radio did not tell. The people who hid them also listened to forbidden foreign broadcasts. They told him what had happened during the past few years. Simon had known America was in the war, but not of the great army and navy and air force America was mobilizing against Japan and Germany and Italy. He had not known that England had defeated Germany in North Africa. Most important, because it directly affected Poland and eastern Europe, he learned that Russia had defeated Germany in the battle of Stalingrad, and the German armies were in full retreat. The avenging Red Army was chasing them closer and closer to German-occupied Poland.

Would Germany stop them? Or would the Red Army pour into Poland? And what would that mean to the few thousand Jews still alive in the concentration camps?

For Simon now learned that Hitler had used Poland as a graveyard dumping ground for Jews from all over Europe. There were concentration camps in Germany and many had died there, but most of the camps were in Poland. Their very names were names of terror: Treblinka, Sobibor, Maidenek, Belzec, Auschwitz–Birkenau. Besides these, and others, there were five hundred slave-labor camps. Jews worked there until their strength gave out and they could be sent to the death camps where the gas chambers waited for them.

In addition, in some towns and cities, Jews were massacred right in the ghettos where they had been forced to live.

What would the coming of the Red Army mean? And the coming of the other Allied forces across the British Channel? Simon Wiesenthal prayed that he could hide out until the day of Germany's defeat.

It was not to be. He was captured by accident. Schieman was away one day when Simon rushed into the basement because the Germans were making a house-to-house search for a man who had killed a German.

Simon was lying in his "grave" under the boards without his guns when he heard the tramp of boots. Something about the way the boards were placed must have made them suspicious; they moved them aside and discovered him. It was June 13, 1944.

He was taken to his old concentration camp and found only a handful of Jews still alive there. The Gestapo came. for him, led by Oscar Waltke, noted for his cat-and-mouse cruelty. Simon knew Waltke would torture him before murdering him, to punish him for his escape. Anything was better than that, even suicide. As Oscar Waltke ordered him to get into a truck Simon Wiesenthal slid a razor blade out of the cuff of his jacket and boldly slashed both his wrists.

Awakening in the hospital, he knew with bitterness that his suicide had failed. He was still alive and he was still Waltke's special prey. He was in the Gestapo's own hospital —the only Jew ever permitted in there. The doctors had orders from Waltke to give Wiesenthal good food so he would quickly recover and see to it he had no chance to kill himself again. Waltke was not going to be denied his sadistic pleasures.

On July 16 Simon was well enough. He was to go to Waltke the next day.

But all night long the heavy guns were pounding from the east, and Red Army planes were flying over Lwow and dropping bombs. The Russians were coming closer and closer. Simon could tell the Germans in the hospital, the doctors and nurses, were nervous. What about the SS men? Were they thinking of their own future? Were they planning to stay and fight?

The next day he was taken back to the concentration camp, along with other Jews, Poles, and Ukranians, who had in some way offended the SS. The others were taken off to be shot but Wiesenthal was brought before the camp commander, a man as brutal as Waltke but more cunning.

Warzok, the commander, made no effort to hide his plans from his SS subordinates—or from Wiesenthal, who stood listening.

Let Waltke stay in Lwow and suffer, said Warzok. The commander and his favorites would take Wiesenthal and all the rest of the Jews in the concentration camp, the thirty-four who were still alive out of the 149,000 Jews who had once lived in Lwow, and use them as an excuse to run to Germany before the Germans came.

They had to have an excuse. The retreating German army was coming close, stopping now and then to fight back at the Russians. If some unpleasant German general found a whole bunch of SS men with nothing to do, he might demand they join the fighting men, or else be denounced as cowards back in Berlin. Commander Warzok had to find a reason why he should get back to Germany as quickly as possible, and the Jews were the answer. They would be prisoners the SS must guard. That was their sacred duty. The Jews could not be left for the Russians—think what stories they might tell!

Warzok gestured at Simon Wiesenthal. Such a man was especially needed. He was strong and fit after his hospital feeding. "We need prisoners who can walk, not ones that will die on our hands," he said.

Mixed in with the hatred Simon felt for the SS, there was now contempt. They were cowards. They didn't care if the German army lost to the Russians; all they wanted to do was save their own skins.

The SS men and their prisoners began a long trek east and south, going from one concentration camp to another. At first it was not too difficult, except for the shortage of food for the Jews. The SS had been for so long such a feared elite among the Germans that Warzok was able to get train space even though it meant putting army men off. He commandeered wagons when there was no other transportation.

He ordered Simon and the other Jews to forget they were Jews. He had gathered up Poles and Ukranians along the way. They were all supposed to be forced-labor Polish prisoners, who were sorely needed for work in German factories. Still, the amount of prisoners was so small there were half a dozen SS men guarding two or three on each wagon.

One day they came to a bridge along which a large German army convoy was slowly making its way. The Russians were so close behind that mortar shells and rockets were being lobbed uncomfortably close. The German army group had to get across and blow up the bridge or be captured.

Warzok cared nothing for that. He had the incredible arrogance to stop the convoy, order them to get off the bridge and off the road so that his wagons could drive first. He and his SS men held submachine guns on the German officers, who were furious but helpless. It was not so much the threat of the guns—they, too,. had guns—but the awe and fear with which they regarded the SS.

Warzok's wagons rolled across the bridge to safety. Then the SS commander ordered the bridge blown up. The army engineer who was forced to detonate the explosive cursed him; it meant the rest of the army convoy was trapped on the other side. Warzok didn't care. The Russians would be checked long enough to let him escape.

Simon had seen how brutal the SS could be towards Jews. Now he saw they could be equally brutal to others. In one Polish village Warzok and his men surrounded a church while the people were at Mass, arrested them and added them to his "prisoners." He needed more, so as to be able to justify his running away from danger. Now his SS men had a lot of people to guard.

They stopped briefly at the Grossrosen concentration camp and there Wiesenthal received some devastating news. Poles from Warsaw were brought to Grossrosen; they told of the terrible fighting and bombing there. One of the Poles talked about his street, Topiel Street, which had been completely wiped out. Cautiously Wiesenthal asked him if he had known Irena Kowalska at Number 5 Topiel. The Pole did, but he added that she was certainly dead. No one had survived on that street.

"Irena Kowalska" was actually Cyla Wiesenthal.

By January 1945 the Russian were coming close to Grossrosen and once again the SS men marched their prisoners on. Now there were no carts for the prisoners. They must walk through the snow and fierce cold. Thousands died, for the SS had added more from Grossrosen. Those who fell, exhausted, were shot by the SS.

They reached Buchenwald camp and here they were put on trucks, but things were no better. They had to stand; there was little or no food; there were 140 prisoners to each truck and men died, held upright by the tightly jammed mass. All the weight which had been put on Simon Wiesenthal's body at the hospital wasted away; he was little better off than any of the others.

On February 7 they arrived at their final destination: the Mauthausen concentration camp in upper Austria. Of the three thousand who had marched from Grossrosen and Buchenwald and Lwow, only twelve hundred were still alive —and those were barely able to make the final steps into the camp.

Simon Wiesenthal was walking—*staggering* would be the better word—beside another prisoner, a Pole, Prince Radziwill. The two men supported each other as best they could but at last they both fell in the snow. They were too weak to get up again; both were close to death by starvation and by freezing.

Suddenly Wiesenthal came back to consciousness to find himself lifted up, with Radziwill, and carried to a truck. The driver had been ordered by the SS to go out and collect all the stiff, frozen corpses that lined the way to Mauthausen camp. Once inside the camp other prisoners were ordered to take the dead bodies to the crematorium to be burned.

Fortunately, those working on this gruesome detail noticed that Wiesenthal and Radziwill were still slightly warm, still breathing. Instead of taking them to the crematorium they smuggled them into the showers, stripped them and turned the water on full force. The shock revived them.

Once again Simon Wiesenthal had been saved and brought back from the brink of death. Still, being alive in Mauthausen was hardly living. There was no food except for a bowl of something called soup which tasted horrible and smelled worse.

The inmates lay on hard wooden bunks. Every morning those who had died in the night were taken away. The rest lay without speaking, without any interest except to survive just one hour longer. But once Wiesenthal had found himself alive when he had thought himself freezing to death, his will asserted itself. He made himself sit up. He made himself talk, and he became acquainted with a Polish trusty, a prisoner like himself, but one with special duties that gave him extra food. When he found out Simon Wiesenthal had been an architect, he began smuggling in small pieces of bread to him on the condition that Wiesenthal would design a coffee house for him in Poland after the war.

The bread made the difference between starvation and staying alive, and the fierce desire for revenge against the murderers of his mother and wife and people kept the spark of willpower burning.

And it couldn't be much longer! There were whispered rumors: the American, the English and the Russian troops were meeting; Berlin had fallen; Hitler was dead.

On May 4, 1945, all the SS guards at Mauthausen suddenly disappeared. The crematorium stopped burning. There was a weird silence. Gone were the harsh voices, the crack of pistol shots, the creaking wheels of the death carts. The only inmates left in Mauthausen were the living corpses. Few of them had strength enough to make a rustle of sound or movement.

But Simon heard something outside. The rumble of motors. He dragged himself off his bunk and managed to stagger out into the courtyard. He knew it was the liberators coming and he wanted to be on his feet to meet them.

The first American tank with the white star drove in. Simon Wiesenthal took a couple of steps forward before his strength gave way and someone in an American uniform picked him up. Even so, he had managed just to touch the white star of the American tank with his fingers before he lost consciousness.

When he recovered he was lying on his bunk, but even during the short time of his faint everything around him seemed changed. The dead had been taken away. Medical men were moving around the rest, checking pulses for the feeble thread of life. There was a wonderful aroma of real food and the smell of disinfectant and medicines.

Someone raised Simon's head and spooned a broth of real meat and potatoes into his mouth. It was too rich for him after a starvation diet, and he threw it up.

But after that he could eat again, as much and as quickly as his shrunken stomach could take. Doctors came with vitamin pills and shots and there were competent, comforting hands to bathe and clean him and feed him. To his dismay he found himself weaker than before the Americans came, but a doctor assured him that was natural. Now he no longer had to fight to live, his body was letting down and giving way. Food and rest would soon build his strength.

At first, freedom was too strange a thing to be believed. The inmates of Mauthausen, the survivors, waited for orders. They could not think about tomorrow, or what their liberty would mean to them.

Then an incident occurred which broke through the apathy filling Wiesenthal's mind. A Polish trusty, who hated Jews, knocked Simon down as he was slowly walking out of the barracks to test his legs. In his weakened state the blow could have killed him. He was urged to report it to the American authorities, so he and several friends went the next day to the camp headquarters. There was a new sign over the door that read: *War Crimes.*

While they waited their turn they could hear questioning going on inside an inner room; then the door opened and a man who had been one of the most brutal of the SS guards came out, followed by a former Jewish prisoner. To Simon's astonishment, he saw the former guard was trembling. He was more than just frightened; he was in terror. And the former Jewish prisoner was now *his* guard!

So the Americans did mean business. They were rounding up former SS men and holding them for trial.

When Simon made his report, the Polish trusty who had struck him was forced to come to him and humbly beg his pardon.

That night Simon Wiesenthal lay on his bunk and thought about what this victory could mean. It was not only that the Germans were beaten. It was now possible that the SS, the real Nazis, would have to answer for their crimes. Only two weeks had gone by since the liberation of the Mauthausen camp but already some of the former officials had been rounded up, stripped of power, arrested. There was a new prisoner-of-war camp established, and Germans were behind the barbed wire now, waiting to be questioned.

But many of the SS had stripped off their uniforms. They were just ordinary prisoners, like the soldiers, as far as the Americans knew. It would take the survivors to identify them. Simon Wiesenthal made up his mind then and there that he was going to work with the War Crimes office.

The very first Americans to enter Mauthausen had seen with their own eyes the evidence of the horrible murders there. They had seen men and women starving to death. They had seen the crematorium and the towering piles of human bones—all that was left of thousands and thousands of men, women, and children.

But the camp had been cleaned up somewhat. Flesh was beginning to clothe the walking skeletons of Mauthausen. The Americans who were now moving in to administer the welfare of the Jews and Poles, and catch the SS criminals, might find the atrocities hard to believe. It would be up to people like Wiesenthal to convince them that these things had happened.

The next day he volunteered to work for the War Crimes office. Kindly, they told him to wait until he was more fully recovered and had put on weight. He weighed only ninety pounds, about half of the weight he had once carried.

Ten days later, after eating well and doing exercises, Simon Wiesenthal became an official member of the War Crimes commission. The Americans quickly recognized his value to them: he was educated, he spoke several languages, and he had been *inside*—he knew the Nazis.

The Americans were busy searching the countryside for escaped Mauthausen guards. Simon's first task was to accompany Captain Tarracusio, who had once taught international law at Harvard University, to a house where a former SS guard named Schmidt was living. He was hiding on the second floor, and Tarracusio sent Wiesenthal up to arrest him.

Schmidt gave no trouble, but as they drove in the jeep to the camp prison, he pleaded for mercy. He had done nothing really wrong; he had only obeyed orders. Furthermore, he had helped many of the concentration camp inmates.

The Captain might have believed him but Simon said: "Yes, you helped the prisoners. I've often seen you. You helped them on their way to the crematorium."

After that Captain Tarracusio took Simon along with him whenever a search or an arrest was to be made. Sometimes the man arrested claimed they had made a mistake; he was not the Muller or Wagner or Schmidt they wanted. He had never been in the SS.

Of course, he was not wearing the uniform. The minute the war was over they had all stripped off those uniforms. Simon ordered him to take off his shirt. The man's claim of innocence was false. There, under his arm, was a tattoo of the jagged lightning insignia of the SS. Simon had known that many were so proud of that symbol that it had been their custom to have it tattoed on their bodies.

The War Crimes office moved to the city of Linz. Here there were far more Jews than just those of the Mauthausen concentration camp. A refugee camp had been set up to help them, but they were free to move about and they flocked into Linz. All of them were searching, all asking questions of each other. Were you in such-and-such a camp? Did you see my wife there? Do you know what happened to my mother, my father, my children? My son's name was Joseph—he was taken away to work near Treblinka—is there anyone here who might have seen him?

The need to help these people was important. Simon Wiesenthal became vice-chairman of a Jewish Committee. In the mornings he worked at the War Crimes office with Americans, and in the afternoons he sat in the Jewish Committee office.

There he compiled lists of names of all the Jews in the refugee camps around Linz, and the names of members of their families. He sent messages to cities and towns all over

Europe, sending them his lists and getting the names of survivors from them. Each day the names he received were distributed and they passed from hand to hand, as eager Jews thronged the Committee office to see if the name of some loved one was written there.

Simon Wiesenthal not only took down names, he wrote down the people's stories. As he did so, he also began to keep his little black book, with the names of the worst of the SS men, the most horrible of the murderers.

Austria and Germany were now divided into four military zones: American, British, French, and Russian, and the Four Powers were united in one purpose: to investigate war crimes and bring the worst criminals to trial.

Hitler, Goebbels, and Himmler were either known to be or presumed dead. However, there were many top Nazis still alive. A special Allied court to try them was to be convened in October in Nuremberg.

Other trials were going on all over, but the Nuremberg trial would be the most important. The presiding judges and the prosecution attorneys were members of all four Allied nations. It was to be a showcase trial. The defendants were well-known: Hermann Goering, president of the Reichstag, head of the German Air Force, and one of the founders of the Gestapo; Joachim von Ribbentrop, Foreign Minister; Alfred Rosenberg, whose anti-Semitic philosophy had spawned the lies that tried to justify the persecution of the Jews; Hans Frank, Governor-General of occupied Poland, where most of the concentration camps were located; and many more leaders such as these.

The Nuremberg trial would consume much money and time as well as the efforts of some of the world's most brilliant legal minds, because this was not only a trial of men but of ideas. The most important question to be resolved was that of responsibility.

All over Germany Nazis were saying "But I only obeyed orders" or "It was all Hitler's fault. I only did what I was told."

If the top Nazis could get off free on such an excuse, then no Nazi or SS man could be tried. They all took orders—but were they forced to? Were they forced to join the SS? Who forced them to torture Jews as well as kill them?

Simon Wiesenthal was determined to be at the Nuremberg trial, but when it opened something happened to delay his appearance there for a while. Another letter came to him. But this one was from Cyla.

His wife was alive!

Chapter Three

Simon's joy was so great he could not work that day. The letter said Cyla was in Cracow, Poland, so he went that very morning to arrange for a travel permit for himself from the Office of Strategic Services. Then, to celebrate, he went to a farm and asked the owner if he could ride a horse for a while. Horseback riding was associated in his mind with his youth, with his engagement to Cyla, with holidays.

Unfortunately, he forgot he was no longer young and was still not very strong. The horse threw him and he broke his ankle.

So now he must lie in bed and try to arrange to get a travel permit for his wife to come from Poland to Austria.

While they waited, they wrote each other. They found that, at the same time he had heard she had been killed in the bombing on Topiel Street, she had heard he had cut his wrists and died a suicide. She had escaped the Warsaw bombing but the Germans had taken her to a forced-labor camp inside Germany where she had been liberated by the British.

When the war ended she had not known what to do or where to go. A friend persuaded her to go back to Lwow.

41

It was possible, after all, that Simon might still be alive, although Cyla had no real hope of this. In Lwow she went to talk to a Dr. Biener. The doctor took one look at her and slammed the door shut. She banged on it, and he finally opened the door again. He was white with shock. "But—but you are dead!" he said.

He had just received a letter from Simon telling him that he was in Linz, but that Cyla had died in the bombing in Warsaw.

There were a lot of red tape, bureaucratic rules and regulations to go through to get Cyla out of Poland and into Austria, but late in 1945, while Simon still lay in bed with his broken ankle, the door of his room opened and there she stood, as lovely as ever. It was a poignant moment as they stared at each other. Both were remembering the last time, when they had touched hands through a barbed wire fence.

Amidst the joy of their reunion, there was sadness. They found that all of the rest of her family and his—eighty persons—had perished. They two were the sole survivors.

They took an apartment in Linz and discussed their future. It would not have been too difficult for them to emigrate to Palestine or to America, and for Simon to re-establish himself as an architect, but this was not what he wanted to do. Cyla understood his feelings and agreed with him. She saw that the work he was doing now was more important. He was helping other Jews find their families and begin new futures, and he was helping bring the SS murderers to trial.

Even before Cyla had come to heal the last bitterness of his own personal experiences, Simon had found he no longer wanted personal revenge. He had lusted to kill Warzok and the others, but they were now no more important to him than any other SS men. Less important, perhaps, when he listened day after day to the stories of other Jews.

He had not been tortured so terribly that his spine would be permanently deformed. He had not had his child torn from his arms and seen an SS guard swing the child by the legs and dash its brains out against a wall. He was not blind, like the youth upon whom the fiendish Dr. Mengele had operated to see if he could change brown eyes to blue. He was not mentally crippled, as were so many Jews, haunted by the terrible things they had seen and endured.

In fact, Simon Wiesenthal came to see that miracles had happened to him, over and over again. He was an intensely religious man, with a strain of mysticism in him. He had been spared. It must be for a purpose.

He knew now that six million Jews and five million other people had died in those concentration camps. Those eleven million cried out to him for justice. He must do his part to avenge them. More than that, he must do his part so that the madness of the Holocaust could not happen again. Never again should men come to power who believed they were the master race with privilege to kill those they thought were of inferior blood.

He was in a unique position to do the job he had chosen. His work for the War Crimes office and the Jewish Committee dovetailed with each other. From each one he got information. To each one he could pass on valuable information. The War Crimes office realized that he knew a great deal more about Nazi crimes and criminals than just what had happened in that particular part of Austria. People told him things, events, names, which were invaluable to War Crimes personnel all over Germany and Austria.

From people like Captain Tarracusio Simon learned legal necessities: get the story while it was fresh in someone's mind, get the facts and dates and places. Make the person swear to a written affidavit. And, if possible, get other witnesses to the same atrocity. Make notes of everything, even if it seems unimportant; keep all documents.

Simon had a special talent for dealing with the thousands of Jews who came to the Jewish Committee office for help. As an architect, he knew no structure was sound if the foundation was not sound. He developed an enormous patience, taking a man or woman back and forth across their stories, sorting out all the confusions until he was certain the basic facts were right.

It was difficult. Many of these people did not want to talk about their experiences. They broke down and cried or became hysterical in the midst of telling of some terrible event. They did not always know the full name of the man who had tortured them; the SS did not introduce themselves to "Jewish swine."

Simon was asked to go to Nuremberg for the big trial. How shrunken and nervous these top Nazi leaders looked now, without their titles, their uniforms, their medals, without a chance to strut for the cameras! Hermann Goering was still arrogant, but the others whined the same excuses Nazis were using everywhere:

"It wasn't my fault." "I knew there were concentration camps, but I didn't know what went on there." "I was a loyal German; I only obeyed orders." "It was all Hitler's fault."

The charges were several:

1. Conspiracy to gain totalitarian control of Germany and conspiracy for foreign aggression

2. Crimes against peace and the violation of international treaties

3. War crimes: the murder and ill-treatment of civilian populations and prisoners of war and enslaving labor from occupied territories

4. Crimes against humanity: murder, extermination, enslavement, brutality, persecution of people on political and racial grounds

The defendants had able lawyers to plead for them, but their own history and actions proved them guilty. Hans Frank, who had been Governor-General of Poland and then of the Netherlands, had even kept a diary all the years before and during the war, and had not destroyed it before capture.

What came out strongly in this trial was that the extermination of the Jews and others was not just the result of an insane hatred or contempt for what Germans called "impure and mongrel peoples." It was also big business. Jewish shops, stores, and factories had been taken over by the SS. Jewish homes became the property of the SS to sell. When Jews were taken to concentration camps they were usually allowed one suitcase apiece. Since they were told they were being resettled, they took in that suitcase whatever small and valuable property they had—money, jewels, coin collections, stamp collections.

At the death camps their suitcases were appropriated by the SS. Then came their clothes; they must go to the gas chambers naked. The SS did not even respect the corpses; rings were taken off dead fingers, gold teeth yanked out of dead mouths; even the long hair of women was cut off. Everything had use. Everything became profit for the very special SS bank account.

This elite corps, responsible directly to Hitler through Goering at first, then through Himmler and his subordinates, such as Adolf Eichmann, had its own private treasury. Where—Wiesenthal wondered—had all that money disappeared to?

He would find out, and very soon.

As the Nuremberg trial unfolded it became obvious that there were only a few of those on trial who were not deeply and knowingly guilty of all four charges against them. Those few were freed. The others received either the death penalty or long years in jail.

The decisions were important ones. No longer could any subordinate claim innocence just because he did only what he was ordered to do. Every person was responsible for his or her own acts. There was always a choice. There was always a moment to say *no* to evil, and some Germans had done so.

Simon Wiesenthal was exhilarated by the end of the trial. However some of his satisfaction left him during a conversation he had in Nuremberg after the trial with a high-ranking German who had been part of German Army Intelligence but who had always opposed the Nazis.

This man warned Wiesenthal that the trial, because of its publicity and because of all the time and money spent on it, might easily prevent other trials of criminals who were not so well known. The world would be satisfied that justice had been done, and turn its attention to other matters. Thus, thousands of murderers would escape. And many, the man claimed, had already escaped.

Wiesenthal could not believe this. The SS men were in hiding, that was true. But they could hardly hope to escape forever. There was chaos now in Europe for people had fled from bombed cities, and many Germans were still in prisoner-of-war camps, but order would be restored one day. How could the SS men hope to escape eventual detection?

"Didn't you ever hear of ODESSA?" the man asked.

Wiesenthal could only think of a Russian seaport with that name.

The man shook his head. ODESSA, he explained, was a secret organization of the SS. The name stood for Organisation der SS-Angehörigen, or Organization of SS Members. Long before the war was over certain preparations had been

made to save SS men from discovery and trial; to set them
up inside or outside Germany with new identities; and to
go on safely with the propaganda of the master race against
the Jews and other "inferiors."

Where had the great treasury of the SS gone?

Some of it which had been in the German Reichsbank
had been taken over by the Allied financial officials. But
before the end of the war the SS had removed vast sums in
cash and gold and jewels and had smuggled it out of the
country into Swiss and Spanish banks. These bank accounts
were under individual names of trusted SS men. Even if
the Allies could find these accounts they could not touch
them. The Allies had no authority over Swiss or Spanish
banks.

It was also suspected that some monies and gold were
buried in secret caves and in sunken chests in lakes, inside
Germany and Austria.

ODESSA also had connections in countries in the Middle
East and in South America which would harbor Nazis.
ODESSA organized routes of "safe" houses and "safe" people
through which SS men could be smuggled outside of Germany to seaports and airfields where they could leave for
their new homes.

It was certain that ODESSA was able to supply these
wanted men with forged passports, new names and nation-
alities, and sufficient money. An ex-Nazi murderer boarding
a plane in Madrid might appear to be nothing but a respectable businessman carrying a (forged) Swiss or French
or Agrentinian passport and a visa properly stamped for
entrance to a new country.

Until he learned of ODESSA Simon Wiesenthal had
seen his job as a temporary one. He would help the various
Allied intelligence services in the best way he could. It
would take some time but eventually the SS men would be

rounded up. In every town and most villages, the people were being questioned. Anyone who could not prove he or she had been just an ordinary German citizen was brought to a prisoner-of-war camp, to await further, in-depth questioning. While they waited they were marched out each day to work, under guard, on rebuilding roads or bridges or clearing away bomb rubble.

Most of these prisoners were ex-soldiers. Hidden among them, certainly, would be former SS men. They could try to escape—but where would they go? They had no papers, no money, no friends.

An organization like ODESSA changed that. At least some would be helped to escape. The hidden SS now had a powerful, wealthy, secret organization behind them. During the war the Nazis had used clever forgers to counterfeit huge amounts of British money. They had planned to smuggle this into England and thus ruin its economy. Those same forgers could now be used to prepare false identification papers and passports.

Bringing the SS to justice was going to be much more difficult. It might take a long time.

Simon Wiesenthal's files took on a new importance. He must discover as many names of SS men as he could, and then gather up every scrap of information about each man: description, personal habits, family and friends. Where was he born? Where was he educated? Old newspapers must be searched for photographs or stories about him. Everything that could possibly be a clue went into the man's files, so that he could be identified and exposed even under a false name.

It was to be a manhunt and a detective job. At times Simon Wiesenthal despaired. The SS had operated in every conquered country. He could not imagine how many thousands of them there were.

He told the War Crimes officers about ODESSA. A few believed him, but many scoffed. They could not believe such cunning from "that bunch of gangsters."

Most of the SS men in Simon's files were simply "missing." They might be dead. They were more likely in hiding or planning their escape. It was essential to Simon to find out more of the workings of ODESSA. It was even necessary to convince the Allies that there *was* an ODESSA.

A brilliant piece of deduction on his part helped convince at least some Allied officers that there were organized escape routes.

Austria was a better hide-out, he reasoned, than Germany. There were mountains and hidden valleys; there were several passes into Italy; there were people friendly to Nazis. He strongly suspected the SS would try to get into Austria. One day he discovered that Germans had applied, under false names, to be hired as drivers of United States Army trucks which carried bundles of the American servicemen's newspaper *The Stars and Stripes* between Munich, Germany, and Salzburg in Austria. These drivers had passes allowing them to cross the border without being stopped or searched. Simon became certain they were carrying more than newspapers in those trucks.

He reported his suspicions to the American authorities in Salzburg. The drivers were questioned; the trucks were searched. No escaping SS men found, but it was obvious that men had been concealed in them. Nothing could be proved. The SS men had been dropped off once they had passed the border and before the trucks reached Salzburg.

Two of the truck drivers were arrested for giving false identities. More important, that particular ODESSA escape route could no longer be used since the newspaper trucks would now be searched at the border.

The American Office of Strategic Services (OSS) had

become most impressed with Simon's work. He could only go on as he had before, except that he worked harder than ever. The files he was accumulating seemed to him so few when he realized how large the SS and its branches of Gestapo and Waffen-SS (special killing groups accompanying regular German troops) had been, but his files were impressive to the Americans. He was called in as an expert witness, not only at the trial of the Mauthausen guards, but at several other trials.

In 1946 he was working for the War Crimes Commission, and also for the U. S. Office of Strategic Services and for the U. S. Counter-Intelligence Corps His name was becoming known outside of Austria. Letters of inquiry came to him from government officials in Holland and Belgium and Czechoslovakia.

All of this hard work took its toll. He slept badly. He had recurring nightmares of the terrible events he had lived through—of the last glimpse of his mother's face—of being naked in the "hose" and waiting for the bullet to strike the back of his head—of lying under the boards in the cellar and hearing the German boots coming closer—of almost freezing to death in the snow at Mauthausen.

So he would get up and sit at his desk and work on his files. For relief, he also began a hobby of stamp collecting; sometimes in the long nights he would work on that. And sometimes he just sat and worried.

By 1946 the first Americans he had met had gone home. Their replacements had never seen the death camps and gas chambers. They were anxious to get Germany back on its feet and restore its economy. Hunting war criminals became secondary. And the new Americans were lenient and easily fooled. They wanted to be *liked*. They were prepared to trust any German who seemed on the surface to be responsible and respectable and friendly.

The Soviets, in their occupying zones of Europe, were not softhearted. The Germans had overrun part of their country and devastated it. Millions of Russians had died. So the Soviets had no mercy, especially on the Waffen-SS. The French, too, were merciless. They had known the cruelty of the SS-Gestapo in their own cities and towns. The British varied a good deal, Simon found. In some of their posts they went grimly after Nazis. In others, they took the attitude that the war was over and it was not sporting to hunt down the defeated.

Simon Wiesenthal had no interest in ordinary German soldiers or civilians. He did not believe all Germans were guilty to the same extent; he remembered well the kindness of Guenthert and Kohlrautz at the Lwow Railway Repair Works.

It was the SS who had committed the worst "crimes against humanity." Simon worried that the Americans, particularly, were beginning to lose sight of this fact.

In the midst of his growing anxieties in that year of 1946 something wonderful happened. A daughter was born to Simon and Cyla Wiesenthal. They named her Pauline. With all their families and relatives dead, this new birth became the symbol of a resurrection from the past, a hope for the future.

Yet Simon did not consider becoming an architect again. His new work had become a crusade.

He had a list of his Most Wanted "clients"— as he called the SS men he sought:

Martin Borman, Hitler's chief Deputy, the man Hitler named to be his successor. It was said Borman had been killed by a bomb in Berlin, but no one could be sure.

Dr. Josef Mengele, chief doctor at Auschwitz concentration camp, who experimented medically upon the inmates, especially on children. If the children survived his tortures they were often crippled, blind, or insane. Dr. Mengele waited for each trainload. He stood by as people disembarked and pointed to this one and that one for his vile experiments.

Dr. Karl Babor, judge and executioner at the Grossrosen camp. Simon had seen him there. The doctor judged each person for work usefulness. "To the left" meant death; and the doctor personally gave those people a lethal injection in their hearts of phenolic acid.

Franz Stangl, commander of the Treblinka camp. Of the seven hundred thousand inmates, only about forty survived.

Kurt Wiese, who had murdered over two hundred Jews in Poland.

Franz Murer, the "Butcher of Wilna," Deputy Kommissar for Wilna, in Esthonia, saw to it that of the eighty thousand Jews who had lived in that city only 250 were left to tell of his atrocities.

Adolf Eichmann.

Simon Wiesenthal had known nothing of Adolf Eichmann when the war ended. Eichmann was not connected with any particular death camp. The Jews who thronged Wiesenthal's office in Linz had no stories to tell of him.

Very soon, however, the Americans found official Nazi files that described the work of Group (sometimes called Bureau) IV, and the head of Group IV was a man called Adolf Eichmann.

Group IV was the executive branch of the SS. This was the planning office, with branches in most major cities of the conquered countries whose sole work was the organization of mass murder. It was run like any business and Adolf Eichmann was its chief executive.

Where was he now?

It was probably easier for Eichmann to hide than many others. He had operated from his office. His face was known only to his office personnel and chief assistants: Erich Rajakowitsch; Rolf and Hans Guenther in Prague; Alois Brunner, who had been in charge of Greece; a man named Hunsche, operating in Budapest; Dannecker in Paris; Seidl and Burger in Theresienstadt; Anton Brunner, who had worked in Vienna.

One of Eichmann's deputies, Dieter Wisliceny, had been caught in Czechoslovakia and sentenced to death. He had supplied the other deputies' names, and also claimed to know where Eichmann was hiding: somewhere in Austria. He didn't know just where.

More information came in to the War Crimes office. Seidl, Dannecker, and Anton Brunner were dead. Simon crossed them off his list. Rolf Guenther was presumed dead. Alois Brunner had escaped from Athens to Damascus, Syria, where he was safe from extradition. Simon kept both those last two names on his active list.

It was by accident that Simon had come across his first real clue to Eichmann. It happened in 1945, before Simon knew that his wife was still alive. He was living in rooms at Landstrasse 40 in Linz, because both the War Crimes office and the Jewish Committee were on that same street. One July night, while he was sitting at his table going over his files and lists of wanted names, his landlady came in to make up his bed. Finished with that, she came to stand behind him and look over his shoulder, glancing down at the names on his list.

"Eichmann!" she exclaimed. "That must be the SS General Eichmann who commanded the Jews."

It was a strange way of describing his work but Wiesenthal understood her and nodded.

"Then," she said, "did you know his parents live on this same street? At Landstrasse 32?"

He was astounded. No one knew that fact at the War Crimes office. No one knew anything of Eichmann's early life, or that he had ever lived in Linz.

The next day he inquired and found there was, indeed, an Eichmann family living on that street. The father owned an electrical appliance store. The War Crimes office was notified and two American officials went to call on the family and searched the house.

They admitted that Adolf was their son and he had been with the SS, but that was almost all the family would admit. The search of the house turned up nothing of any use—no letters, no photograph of Adolf. Finally, the family did say that they had heard from Adolf a few months ago and the message had come from Prague in Czechoslovakia. The only biographical facts they grudgingly gave were that their son had been born in Germany but brought to Linz in Austria when he was small, and that he had married and had three children.

Where were the wife and children? Eichmann's father and mother said they did not know. This might be the truth. Adolf Eichmann might be clever enough to cut off any connection between his parents and himself and his wife.

At least the information corrected many false rumors. It had been said that Eichmann was a German born in Palestine, and that he spoke Hebrew and Yiddish fluently—which he did not. It had been said he was dead. Now, at least, they knew Eichmann had been alive and in Prague recently.

The War Crimes Commission and the Office of Strategic Services concluded there was nothing else to be learned through the family in Linz. But Captain Eugene O'Meara of the OSS asked Simon to concentrate on tracing Eichmann. He issued Simon a highly unusual pass which enabled him to go and come as he chose. It read:

"TO WHOM IT MAY CONCERN:

"The bearer *Ing. Wiesenthal, Simon* is working on confidential investigative work for this organization. Kindly let him move freely in American-occupied Austria, and in case of any inquiries please contact this office."

EUGENE F. O'MEARA
Captain, CAC
Commanding Officer.

For a long time, however, only bits and scraps of information about Eichmann came Simon's way. The man was well protected or well hidden.

In 1947 Simon Wiesenthal opened his own Documentation Center in Linz. He worked *with* the Americans and *with* the Jewish Committee, but he was setting up on his own. He needed to be free of other demands to concentrate on amassing information about war criminals, particularly Eichmann.

In the search for that man, he was sometimes led to others.

Chapter Four

One night Simon was awakened in his apartment by a loud knock on the door. He started up in fright. Even after several years of freedom, old terrors came back at night. It was the knock on the door which so often had heralded the coming of the Gestapo, and Jews had lived with that fear so long they reacted instinctively.

But as soon as he was awake he remembered: this was 1947. He had no reason to fear the nights. He opened his door to three men who identified themselves. They were Jews who had been partisan guerrillas fighting in Russia during the war against the Germans. Their families had been murdered in Poland; the three of them were now living in Austria.

Like Simon, they were on the lookout for former Nazis, and they were convinced they had found out where Eichmann was hiding.

Where?

In Styria, they told him, in that northwest corner of Austria, an area of mountains and valleys and lakes. There they had heard of a prosperous chicken farmer, a man whom neighbors whispered had once been a big Nazi, and who was known to hate Jews most bitterly. It *could* be Eichmann! Simon was not convinced. He was sure Eichmann was too clever to live so openly and give himself away to his neighbors, but there was no harm in going to Styria to see. The chicken farm was in the British zone so they had to get permits. When they arrived in the nearest village, they also had to ask assistance from the Austrian police, since neither Simon Wiesenthal nor the other three had official status. At the field police post in Gaishorn an elderly policeman listened to their description of the chicken farm and nodded his head.

"Must be Gaishorn 66," he said. "Belongs to Murer. He was in Poland and Russia during the war. He's very popular around this village."

"Murer?" Weisenthal gasped. "Franz Murer?"

"That's right," said the old man.

Simon and the others walked out, stunned. This was not Eichmann, but a criminal almost as bad, almost as much sought after. *Franz Murer*—the Butcher of Wilna. Of the eighty thousand Jews who had lived in Lithuania before the war, now there were only about two hundred fifty left living. This was the work of Franz Murer.

And here he had been in Austria ever since the war, a placid, respectable chicken farmer—"very popular around this village," as the policeman described him. How could it have happened?

It wasn't hard to figure out. This was not a well-populated area; it mountains and valleys made for good hiding places. The farmers were clannish. Most of them had liked the Nazi ideas. They hated Jews and were suspicious of foreigners, particularly those who had conquered them. They would never tell the British anything. They would protect someone like Murer, who was to them a good Austrian. He probably drank beer with them on Saturday nights and was a prosperous man who gave employment to others. Simon Wiesenthal knew he would have to act fast or they would hide Murer away.

Not far away was Camp Admont for displaced persons who had not yet found a home to go to. There were Jews there and among them there were survivors of the Wilna concentration camp. Simon and the three others drove to Camp Admont. They got permission to use the loudspeaker and, over it, they asked for any Wilna survivors to come forward.

There were seven. When they heard that Franz Murer was living and prospering so close to them, their emotions were terrible. Some cried, some became hysterical. Memories they had been trying to forget surged upward and their stories poured out between sobs and gasps.

They remembered the day Murer had ordered the Jews of one street in the city of Wilna to be loaded into trucks and driven to a nearby wood, where they were shot one after another by his special Lithuanian police. One Jew had survived to tell of the slaughter.

Another time Murer had ordered two houses in a Jewish street dynamited. There were still people inside but that did not stop him.

Wilna had formerly been a center of well-to-do and intellectual Jews, who had fine collections of silver and porcelain and paintings and jewelry. Murer enjoyed bargaining with the Jews—their collections for their lives—and then, once everything valuable was delivered to him, laughing at them, beating and torturing them with his own hands, and finally killing them.

One story was especially awful. Two groups of men waited at the concentration camp gate; one group to be marched to slave work, the other to the woods to be shot. In the latter group was seventeen year-old Daniel Brodi. At the last moment he ran to the work group to say goodbye to his father. Franz Murer saw him, struck him down and then shot him in the head so that the boy fell dying at his father's feet.

Wiesenthal took down all the stories and had them notarized. It was difficult because the Wilna survivors were so emotional it was hard to pin them down to dates and times and places, and to name other witnesses to the same incidents. When he got as much as he could from Camp Admont Simon went to the police, and accompanied them to the chicken farm.

But someone must have tipped Murer off. He was ready to leave, with suitcases already packed. When he was arrested, he was rude and arrogant.

He had reason to be unworried. The British were not nearly as anxious to prosecute a Franz Murer as they were to find out what Simon Wiesenthal was doing in their zone. At that time they were doing their best to prevent Jews—such as were at Camp Admont—from emigrating to Palestine, and they were certain that Simon Wiesenthal was just using his Documentation Center as a cover to help smuggle Jews out of Europe into Palestine. One Nazi more or less didn't matter. Their suspicions were on Wiesenthal, instead.

Their interrogation of Simon became so outrageous that crowds of Jews from Camp Admont gathered outside headquarters to demand Simon be let go. They shouted in fury, and Simon was released.

Murer was now in prison, but there were rumors that he, too, was going to be released. Simon got in touch with the staff of the International Military Tribunal in Nuremberg which warned the British to hold Murer where he was until it could be determined where he would be tried.

In December of 1948 Murer was extradited to the Russians. This was normal procedure since his crimes had been committed in what was now the territory of the Soviet Union.

There was a trial and Murer was found guilty and sentenced to twenty-five years at hard labor.

The sentence might have been death, but almost all the evidence came from the affidavits Simon Wiesenthal sent. None of the witnesses was willing to go to the Soviet Union to testify. The father of the dead young Daniel Brodi absolutely refused. He wanted only to go to America and forget.

Forget! It was not only Jews who wanted to forget. The British had their problems. The French occupation forces were eager to go home and rebuild the shattered economy of their own country, so long occupied by the Germans. The Americans had their hands full with immediate problems in their zones: with the black market; with organizing local police and town functionaries among Germans whose records were reasonably clean; trying to help displaced persons; getting roads rebuilt, schools started, cities cleaned of bomb rubble.

There was also a growing coolness between the Soviet Union and the rest of the Allies. Simon found the Americans much more concerned with the growth of Communism than the revival of Nazi ideas.

Sometimes he felt as if no one cared any longer about bringing the SS to justice. He had to go on caring, even if no one else did.

In August of that year one of his friends came to him with the rumor that Eichmann was hiding in Fisherdorf, a suburb of the village of Altaussee. He doubted the tip was worth anything. Eichmann had been reported in one place after another, and always the reports had been wrong.

But Altaussee was a remote village in the mountains, beside a lake. It could be a good hideout.

Wiesenthal's friend even gave him the number of a house in Altaussee: No. 8 on Fisherdorf street. Simon telephoned the American authorities in the region where Altaussee was located. They asked the Austrian police to investigate. Whether by an honest mistake or by a deliberate attempt of the Austrians to help "one of our own" they went to Number 38 instead of Number 8. Naturally the appearance of the police on the street asking for Eichmann alerted the other residents.

By the time the police did go to the right house, there was no Eichmann there.

There *was*, however, a Frau Veronika Liebl who admitted that she had been Eichmann's wife but was now divorced from him and had not seen him since their divorce in Prague in March of 1945. She stated she was living quietly in Altaussee with her three boys and she knew nothing more of Eichmann and wanted no trouble from anyone.

It sounded as if it could be true. Neither the Americans nor Austrians had any reason to arrest her. They had no valid reason to doubt her word.

Wiesenthal doubted it very much. He called on local hotels in the area and found Eichmann had stayed at the Parkhotel around May 1. The woman who owned the hotel talked freely to him, but when the American authorities questioned her later she would not talk. Someone had ordered her not to reveal anything about Eichmann. Frau Liebl also claimed she knew nothing about her ex-husband being at the hotel.

This is where Simon Wiesenthal showed his special flair for detective work. Even in the hostile atmosphere of Altaussee he could get some people to say more to him than they meant to. With his patience and persistence he wore down their resistance.

He found several people who admitted they had seen Eichmann and other SS men in May, in a convoy of trucks. One thought the group had unloaded many boxes in an inn barn. Wiesenthal questioned the innkeeper, who said it was true but that he had been warned not to touch them. Then the boxes disappeared; he did not know when. Simon wondered if it could have been SS loot in those boxes.

By 1947, after Captain O'Meara had asked him to take over full responsibility for the finding of Eichmann, Simon already knew a great deal. He had traced Eichmann from Prague to Austria. Anton Burger, an arrested SS man, had stated definitely he had once seen Eichmann in Altaussee.

Now Simon met with a member of the Nuremberg trial staff who showed him a copy of the interrogation of a Rudolf Scheide. Scheide had been in a prisoner-of-war camp at the end of 1945. He had met another prisoner there who called himself Eckman. Scheide became suspicious and confided to the authorities that he thought it was Eichmann. The next day prisoner Eckman was gone. He had been working with a construction gang which was allowed to leave the camp. He had gone out with them that morning and simply had not returned.

Scheide was positive Eckman was really Eichmann. The description fitted. By now, from the parents, Simon had a general description: slender, not very tall, a receding hairline, dark-haired, no distinguishing marks. Unfortunately, it was a picture that could be true of thousands of men. It was one reason Eichmann was so hard to find.

His trail was like a weasel's. He slipped in and out of places, leaving only the faintest of spoor behind him. First Prague, then Bohemia, then Altaussee, then back to Germany into and out of a prisoner-of-war camp. Where would he have gone now? Simon clung to the thought of Altaussee. The ex-wife's house was the only fixed location.

But no new tips were coming in. Simon had to try other avenues. One would be women. Many of the top Nazis had mistresses as well as wives. Perhaps Eichmann had, too. Simon questioned Dieter Wisliceny, who was waiting for his death sentence to be carried out and eager to talk, hoping for reprieve. "Did Eichmann have mistresses?" asked Simon. Wisliceny said yes, and gave a list of women's names.

Several of the women were located. To get them to talk would be a delicate matter so Wiesenthal asked a very handsome Jew, Manus Diamant, to help. Manus could pass for a Hollander so he was given a Dutch name "Herr von Diamont," and a false identity as a former Dutch SS man who had worked with the German SS.

"Herr von Diamont" went to visit several of Eichmann's women—including his divorced wife. He had no luck whatsoever with Frau Liebl, who simply wouldn't talk about her former husband, but he was more successful with a girl who lived in a suburb of Linz.

He beguiled the girl with his good looks and persuaded her of his Nazi sympathies. They spent an evening going over her picture album—and she pointed proudly to one as being that of her lover, Eichmann! She didn't want him to take the picture but he talked her into it; he so much admired Herr Eichmann that he wanted to have a copy made for himself.

With the photograph in front of him, Wiesenthal at last knew exactly what Eichmann looked like.

He wasn't bad looking. If it wasn't for the cold, cold eyes and the mouth, it could have been a pleasant face with absolutely nothing remarkable about it. The picture had been taken when he was young, so he probably had less dark hair now in 1947. Scheide had said Eichmann was going slightly bald in front. The face was slender and oval; the bones might be a little sharper now.

If, thought Wiesenthal, you just gave the portrait a quick glance, it could be the picture of any bookkeeper or store clerk or bank teller.

The eyes and the mouth were something else. It wasn't just because he knew Eichmann was cold-blooded that Wiesenthal read the merciless look in those eyes—it was there. And the mouth was strange. The bottom lip might show some sensuality, but the top one was a straight, hard, determined slash.

It was the face of a young man of some intelligence, no humor at all, but of a young man absolutely resolute to get to the top—or, at least, as far as his abilities would take him. Nor would it make any difference in the world to him whether the "top" was a top executive in a legitimate business company or a top executive in the business of murder.

Not long after Wiesenthal got this picture, he also received a call from the same American agent who had helped him before. Could Simon come to Bad Ischl immediately? It was urgent.

Bad Ischl was a town not far from Altaussee. When the two men met, the American informed Wiesenthal that Frau Veronika Liebl had applied to the local court to declare her husband dead.

It was not an unusual request at that time. So many husbands and wives were missing in the bombed-out, rubble-strewn towns and cities that the courts were beseiged by people wanting such an official declaration. Without it they had difficulty using bank accounts or selling property or settling estates or making wills or marrying again. The courts were usually willing to oblige, but they had to have some proof or strong evidence of death.

What was the "proof" of Eichmann's death? The court judge told the American agent that a Karl Lukas who lived in Prague had sent in an affidavit (sworn testimony) that he had been present on April 30, 1945, when Adolf Eichmann was shot and killed during the fighting in Prague at the end of the war.

The American agent, armed with all that Wiesenthal had told him, informed the judge the affidavit had to be a lie; that Eichmann had been seen alive after April of 1945, both in Prague and in Austria. Shocked, the judge agreed to withhold action on the application until proof could be obtained from Wiesenthal.

He and the American went to work to get the necessary proofs from witnesses who had seen Eichmann, but Simon Wiesenthal felt this was not enough. After all, it would just be the word of men like Scheide and some of the people around Altaussee against the word of this man Karl Lukas. One of Wiesenthal's friends was sent to Prague.

Nine days later the whole trick was exposed. Karl Lukas was married to Maria Lukas—and her maiden name was Liebl! She was the sister of Eichmann's wife. The whole family was in on the conspiracy. Once Adolf Eichmann was declared officially dead the search for him would be over and he would be forgotten. It was a clever trick, and must certainly have been arranged between Eichmann, his ex-wife, and her family.

The judge was outraged. He denied Frau Liebl's application. Officially, Eichmann was still listed as alive.

As a matter of fact, the trick backfired. The attempt to prove Eichmann dead only raised strong suspicions that he was very much alive—and that his wife and her family knew it. Wiesenthal had suspected all along that the divorce had been just a legal device so that the wife could claim she was a private citizen with no ties to Eichmann; that she could escape with just a minimum of questioning; and that she would be free to live quietly and unmolested.

She and Eichmann had been extremely clever and careful. The American authorities, for a long while, had intercepted her mail and monitored her phone calls, and had finally given up because there seemed to be absolutely no communication between them.

Today, Simon Wiesenthal feels that: "The most important thing I was able to contribute to the search for Eichmann was destroying the legend of his alleged death. Many SS criminals will never be caught because they have had themselves declared dead, and have lived happily ever after under new names. . . ."

In 1948 the Americans found Eichmann's personal and office files. Simon Wiesenthal went to the central War Crimes office in Nuremberg and studied photocopies of these files. There were also two photographs.

The one in the black SS uniform with its silver forked lightning insignia interested Wiesenthal. The smart officer's cap gave to Eichmann's commonplace face a swashbuckling character. But, compared with the other youthful picture Wiesenthal had seen before, Eichmann had acquired a foxy look as if he now knew how clever he was. The bones had sharpened.

Here, too, was the true biography of the man. Eichmann had gone to public school in Linz, and then spent two years at the Federal School for Electrical Engineering. From 1925 to 1927 he had been a salesman at the Upper-Austria Electrical Company; from there he became the representative of the Vacuum Oil Company in Vienna. He was fired—because they found out he had secretly joined the Nazi Party.

Eichmann had written his biography in his own hand. "I joined the Austrian NSDAP [*the Austrian Nazi Party*] on April 1, 1932, and also joined the SS," he had stated. "On August 1, 1933, I was ordered by the Gauleiter of Upper-Austria . . . to start my military training at camp Lechfeld [*this was SS training, not regular army*]. On September 29, 1933, I was assigned to the SS liason office Passau. On January 29, 1934, I was ordered to join the Austrian SS in Camp Dachau. On October 1, 1934, I was transferred to . . . Berlin, where I am now on duty."

(Signed) Adolf Eichmann
SS Haupscharfuhrer

1934. It was around then that Eichmann had deliberately and shrewdly chosen the "Jewish question" as the field where he could study and become an expert and advance himself. Hitler, Himmler, Goebbels, Rosenberg and all the other big-shot Nazis were raving and ranting against the Jews; very well, that would be a good subject for a young, ambitious Eichmann to study. The Party had plenty of politicians and propagandists, but they did not have the efficiency experts.

If Hitler really meant to transport all the Jews out of Germany, or kill them—it didn't matter to Eichmann which it was!—he was determined to make himself the man for the job. He'd never had any personal unpleasant experiences with Jews; in his younger days he was not particularly anti-Semitic. In later years he did, indeed, glory in the millions he had destroyed, but it probably would have made no difference to him if they had been Jews or Chinese or Welshmen.

Studying Eichmann's letters and his biography, Wiesenthal could almost think his way into the other's brain.

Eichmann did study a little of the Jewish religion and history. It was not profound research but it didn't have to be. The other Nazis were content to believe all the mixed-up trash that Goebbels spewed out: Jews were inferior, but

Jews were too smart; they were clannish, yet they were trying
to intermarry and mongrelize the pure Aryan blood; they
were all rich bankers, yet they were all poor Bolsheviks;
world Jewry controlled the newspapers, the stock markets
and the governments of the democracies, yet Jews were
slavish by nature. In such an atmosphere Eichmann's meager
knowledge passed as sound scholarship.

The first test given him was to supervise the destruction
of the Viennese synagogues. Though not a man of action,
he organized it so well that he was picked to organize the
first concentration camp set up in conquered Czechoslovakia.

To the Nazis, the camp became a model to admire; to
the Jews, it was a place of desperate horror. The President
of the Jewish Community in Prague protested to Eichmann
the orders sending Jews to the camp. Jews had lived as
good citizens in Czechoslovakia for a thousand years. Eichmann only said: "I'll show you!"—and the President and
other Jewish dignitaries were the first inmates of the concentration camp.

When the Wannsee Conference was held, at which the
"Final Solution" was decided upon, Adolf Eichmann was
the natural choice to carry out the orders of Hitler and
Himmler and Heydrich. Eichmann, presumably, knew how
Jews would behave; he knew how to get things done; he
was already studying the merits of burning Jews in crema-
toriums or gassing them with cyanide tablets. He was a man
who did things thoroughly, efficiently.

Simon Wiesenthal was not at all certain he would ever
find Eichmann. Eichmann was clever and methodical. Still,
even the clever ones made mistakes.

Chapter Five

While keeping an eye on Altaussee and Eichmann's wife, Simon had other "clients" to attend to. One of these was Franz Stangl.

Simon had come across the name while reading a list of decorations awarded to SS men. Franz Stangl had received an amazing number of such honors, and they were for "special merit in the technique of mass extermination."

Stangl had been commandant of the Treblinka death camp. As such, he was responsible for the treasure shipped to swell the bank account of the SS. A document was discovered which was Stangl's report of a shipment back to Germany:

> 25 freight cars of women's hair
> 248 freight cars of clothing
> 100 freight cars of shoes
> 22 freight cars of dry goods
> 46 freight cars of drugs
> 254 freight cars of rugs and bedding
> 400 freight cars of various used articles
> 2,800,000 American dollars

400,000 pounds sterling
12,000,000 Soviet rubles
140,000,000 Polish zlotys
400,000 gold watches
145,000 kilograms golden wedding rings
4,000 karats of diamonds over 2 karats
120,000,000 zlotys in various gold coins
Several thousand strings of pearls.

(Signed) *Franz Stangl.*

All of this, destined for the SS treasury, had been taken from the bodies of victims.

Simon traced Stangl to his last SS post in Yugoslavia. After being two years a prisoner of war he had slipped away to Damascus, Syria. When Stangl learned that Simon Wiesenthal knew he was there, he ran again—this time to Brazil.

South America had always had large colonies of Germans and they had prospered there. They had ties to South American politicians, and ODESSA made good use of this. Simon had discovered that Dr. Mengele was already there; now Stangl had joined him. And how many others? Many South American countries refused to deport Nazis, no matter what official requests were made that they be returned to stand trial.

It was bitter for Simon Wiesenthal to realize that so many of the worst Nazis were probably living comfortably there, spreading their Nazi doctrines.

He decided to bring ODESSA out into the open. He wrote newspaper and magazine articles. They did not attract much attention at that time, but another story he wrote was a sensation. This was the expose of Castle Hertheim.

Castle Hertheim was located not far from the concentration camp of Mauthausen. While Simon was still a prisoner there he had heard the name. One of the crematorium ovens, running full blast day and night, broke down. Experts were brought to fix it. It was said they came "from Hertheim." And during the trial of the Mauthausen guards, one mentioned that he had come to the camp "from Hertheim."

But what was it? It was empty now.

Digging into Nazi files, Simon found out that the castle had been used during the war as a euthanasia center: that is, a place to kill off the Germans the Nazis felt were unfit to live—the old and insane and incurably ill. Hitler had proclaimed the Germans to be the master race. These poor unfortunates were an embarrassment to him. They only showed how human the Germans were, prone to the same ills as other people.

So Castle Hertheim was one of the killing centers for these people.

It was also something else. It was a training center for the very young, new SS recruits. Simon had found that an enormous number of such young men had spent time at Castle Hertheim, far more than were necessary to kill a few old or insane or ill people. No, they had been sent there to *watch*. In this way they became hardened to murder, and indifferent to brutality.

They were taught that this was their duty, and an honorable thing. No weakling, afraid to see others die, was fit to wear the glorious SS uniform.

Undoubtedly some of the new recruits could not take it. They were weeded out. Only those who could force themselves to forget all their childhood lessons of humanity and brotherhood and compassion for others could last through the training of Castle Hertheim.

It explained something that puzzled many people. In the SS were thousands and thousands of men; how was it possible that so many Germans and Austrians could be of such a cruel nature? Was it something inherent in the German blood? Simon had never believed this. He could see that the SS training twisted them.

Certainly there were brutes in the SS, men who so enjoyed brutality that the only explanation for them was that they had joined the SS *because* they were that way. For the rest, all that had been good in them was twisted into a fanatical devotion to Hitler, and a comradeship among themselves.

So Simon wrote the story. People who had been saying he was only a vengeful Jew who hated all Germans and Austrians, were forced to shut up.

Simon Wiesenthal's growing reputation as a writer came during the years 1948 and 1949. He helped support himself and his family and the Documentation Center in that way.

When he had written about the SS and their huge bank accounts and loot, various anonymous people had written to the newspapers demanding to know where Wiesenthal got his money, and hinting he was supported by sinister "Jewish international capitalists." This was totally untrue. When the Documentation Center opened he had unpaid assistants. He received fifty dollars a month from one man and Simon made up the balance of expenses by writing. In the 1950's West Germany agreed to pay restitution to Jews for losses of property. For a long time Simon refused to take anything, but at last he reluctantly did, spending far more than half of it on the work of the Documentation Center.

In later years he organized the Federation of Jewish Victims of the Nazi Regime. The twelve hundred members contribute voluntarily what they can, sometimes one dollar, some months nothing, sometimes as much as a hundred dollars. Holland set up a special Wiesenthal Fund, and so have groups in many cities. The money goes to the work and can be spent only when authorized by four officials of a special committee.

In 1949 Simon was not thinking of money. He was thinking of Eichmann. Two years had gone by without sight or sound of him.

Then, on December 20, a high-ranking police officer from the Altaussee district came to Simon and said he had news of Eichmann. Frau Liebl and her three sons were still living there. The policeman believed Eichmann was somewhere in the same area, and very likely living near Grundlsee, a village only a couple of miles away. A "see" was a lake. Grundlsee had only a few, very scattered and lonely and hidden houses along its shores. But a Mercedes automobile had been glimpsed there. It was unusual enough to excite interest. The local inhabitants could not afford such a car.

Simon was excited. "Only recently," he explained to the policeman, "a friend of mine in that area also reported the sight of a black Mercedes in Altaussee—and it stopped in front of Frau Liebl's house!"

Simon did not have many friends in that area. In fact, it amazed him that this policeman should be on his side. The hostility of most of the Altaussee people towards Simon had made his task very difficult. He was certain that his appearance in the village caused alarm, and that Frau Liebl was told immediately that "*that* Wiesenthal is here again!" He was also certain that former SS men and their families and sympathizers were well-organized in that area.

A police official who would voluntarily come to Wiesenthal's Documentation Center to inform on Eichmann was a rare and good person. He urged Wiesenthal to move quickly; New Year's eve was approaching and there was every reason to believe that Eichmann would be spending New Year's with his former wife and his sons.

Simon's own birthday was New Year's eve. What better

present could he have than the capture of Eichmann? He and the policeman laid their plans most carefully, most secretly.

Unfortunately, he had another visitor the next night. A young Israeli, who had fought for Israel's independence, was on a trip to Europe and called in to visit the famous Simon Wiesenthal. He had never known any of the Nazi terrors, for his family had emigrated to Palestine when he was very young, but he was intensely interested in the work of the Documentation Center. When Wiesenthal told him of Eichmann and the immediate possibility of arresting such a man, the young Israeli was on fire to go with him.

What a tremendous thing it would be for him, an Israeli, to take part in the capture of such a murderer of the Jewish people.

Simon Wiesenthal said no, at first, then he weakened. It seemed to him, too, that it was highly appropriate that this boy, who had fought to make Israel a nation, should be able to return to Israel to tell everyone of his part in getting Eichmann.

They left Linz, and on December 28 they were in Bad Aussee, only a short distance from Altaussee. Simon warned the Israeli that nothing would happen until New Year's eve, and he was not to go wandering about or talking to anyone. He was to stay in the hotel room.

Simon Wiesenthal conferred with the Austrian policeman in secret. He was told that the policeman had men posted around the area at different inns, keeping a watch on the road for a black Mercedes. Then Wiesenthal went to bed.

He did not know that the Israeli, young and sociable and full of excitement, could not sleep and found the loneliness of his room intolerable. Outside the windows of his room he could see lighted taverns and nightclubs and

he could hear the singing and the Christmas week cele-
brations and he could not resist them. He went out, intend-
ing just to have a beer and watch the happy crowds.

The Austrian folk are hospitable, especially on such occa-
sions. They invited the solitary young man to join them.
He did. He was careful to say nothing at all of Wiesenthal
or Eichman, but he could not help boasting that he was an
Israeli and had fought in the war of independence for
Israel. His listeners were fascinated.

Undoubtedly some of them were genuinely interested
and admiring, and they spread the word throughout the
town that there was a real Israeli fighter having a drink
with them. Come and listen to his stories!

There were others who joined to listen, and wonder with
suspicion. What was an Israeli doing here in this remote
part of Austria? Had he come alone, or had someone brought
him? For what reason? There was a mystery here. The word
traveled swiftly from person to person, from house to house,
from village to village.

The young Israeli suspected nothing of the questions he
was arousing. He went home and to bed, saying not a word
to Wiesenthal of his evening.

On the morning of December 31 Simon met again with
the police officer to go over their arrangements. They
seemed to be airtight. All the policemen's men were to be
on duty by nine o'clock that night, stationed at inns and
on all the roads going in to Altaussee. They could not
possibly miss seeing a black Mercedes; they were to let it
pass into the town and notify the police official. Then when
Eichmann reached his ex-wife's house the trap would be
sprung.

At ten o'clock that night Wiesenthal and the police
official made the rounds, checking to see that everyone was
in place and that telephone communications were working.

It was bitterly cold. By the time Simon and the policeman got back to the hotel, which had been established as a sort of headquarters to which the men would telephone, they were badly in need of something hot to drink so they went into the hotel tavern.

There sat the young Israeli, the center of a large group of local people who were listening eagerly to his stories of the Israeli war.

He had been told, once again, to stay in his room, but he had disobeyed. He had seen no harm in it. Both the policeman and Simon were furious with him, but there was nothing they could do about it now. Anyway, it was after ten and Eichmann would be coming soon. Surely nothing could really go wrong!

But as they left the tavern and proceeded to check in at other inns and talk to the men posted there, they found out that everyone was talking about the Israeli. In such quiet little backwater places as Bad Aussee and Altaussee people had little new to gossip about, and the advent of a stranger from Israel was exciting.

Simon Wiesenthal began to feel sick.

Eleven o'clock passed. There was no sign of a black Mercedes in Altaussee. Then, at eleven-thirty, a detective came running to report to the Austrian policeman. He had been stationed, hiding behind trees, on the road coming from Grundlsee. He had watched two men come walking along that road towards Altaussee. He had Eichmann's description and was peering through the trees to see if he could recognize him, when suddenly, as they neared his hiding place, another man rushed down the road *from* Altaussee yelling "Go back! Go back!" Without a moment's pause they turned and ran back the way they had come, towards Grundlsee.

Wiesenthal and the police officer looked at each other,

and both knew the truth. That had been Eichmann and a friend, and they had lost him. Undoubtedly he had his car nearby. It was futile to hunt for him; by now he was miles and miles away, and safe with his "friends."

The police officer tried to console Wiesenthal by assuring him the houses in Grundlsee would be watched carefully from now on. But it was unlikely the clever Eichmann would stay there now that he knew he had been detected. The officer also tried to say it was not the fault of the young Israeli—but both knew better.

For a full week the Austrian police combed the Grundlsee area, with search warrants, but there was no trace of Eichmann or his car. Wiesenthal had a deep foreboding that Eichmann had become frightened enough to give up any hope of hiding forever in Austria and living there under a new identity.

By now he would have taken advantage of the ODESSA escape routes and left Europe entirely. He could be heading for the Middle East or South America, and Wiesenthal feared Eichmann would find the same sanctuary as Stangl and Mengele and others. The last chance of getting Eichmann had been muffed, Wiesenthal thought. There would not be another.

He was wrong—but years would pass before the next chance came.

Chapter Six

The next years were not lucky ones for a Nazi hunter.

Instead of the cooperation that had existed between the Allies immediately after the end of the war, there had come the division called the Cold War. There was suspicion and mistrust, especially between the United States and the Soviet Union. The Soviet Union entrenched its influence over Poland, Czechoslovakia, Rumania and the other Balkan states. America hastened to rebuild the economy of Germany and Austria and Italy, so they could become buffer states between NATO (the North Atlantic Treaty Organization) and Russia.

In 1949 the new Federal Republic of Germany was created while another Germany was being created in the Soviet zone.

America and Britain and France had other problems besides catching the SS murderers. In fact, the need for reestablishing order and discipline inside Germany and Austria was urgent. It was easy to give the jobs of running town administration and the legal system to men of experience, even though those men had been judges and mayors who were members of the Nazi Party and carried out Nazi orders during the war. To add to Wiesenthal's depression and frustration, his informants confirmed his worst fears: Eichmann had left Europe and no one knew where he had gone.

The Wiesenthals moved to Vienna, and Simon established his Documentation Center there. It was in a building hastily put up after the war, and already becoming shabby. There were just two small rooms, in front, and then a narrow hallway which led to Simon's office at the back. All the rooms had bare, cement floors. The Center could not afford the luxury of carpets. There were desks and a few chairs, but the important features were the file cabinets and the shelves. Here was stored, numbered, and indexed, all the material Simon had gathered so patiently.

An old, battered sofa and a wall of bookshelves were the only features that distinguished Simon's private office. He had begun collecting books on the SS, in many languages, until now he had an impressive library on the subject. The sofa was for his visitors, but occasionally Simon stretched out on it for a brief rest. Although he was generally in good health and worked long, long hours, he suffered sometimes from the effects of the beatings he had endured.

Once, when he went for a medical checkup, the doctor asked him if he had been a prize fighter in his youth. The lumps and scars and welts on his body were those of a man who had taken severe punishment; the doctor had seen something like them on the bodies of boxers.

The Documentation Center's principal reason for existence was the correspondence that flowed in and out of its rooms. The results went into the files.

Even before he had his own Center, Simon had begun his systematic network of correspondents. He had personally interviewed the Jewish survivors around Linz, but right after the war the Allies had set up two hundred temporary displaced-persons camps in Germany and Austria. He wanted the same information from the one hundred thousand survivors living in them, before they scattered and found permanent homes.

So he established his network of helpers in each one of those camps and instructed them to interview everyone they could. They were to get accounts of what went on in each particular ghetto or concentration camp; instances of SS brutality; eyewitness stories of killings and torture. They were to get the names and descriptions of the SS men responsible and exact dates and times and places. Then they were to sign the affidavits and send them to Simon Wiesenthal.

In turn, he furnished the War Crimes offices with these documents. They were used at the big Nuremberg trial, the Mauthausen trial, and many others. Many times they had clinched the case against an SS man.

Just filing the affidavits was not enough. Simon studied each one. If a name was mentioned he went to his card indexes and checked to see—yes! It was the same man, the same date, the same place. Now he had two witnesses, more than twice as valuable in a courtroom.

By now, through Simon's efforts, hundreds of SS men had been arrested and brought to trial. But there were thousands and thousands of them. In his files, alone, he had the names of 22,500. But times had changed.

Germany was receiving Marshall Plan aid from America and its economy was being rebuilt. Something else was being rebuilt: those who had been Nazis or Nazi sympathizers were growing bold again. They were going back into business or getting themselves reappointed judges. They were publishing newspapers.

ODESSA, Simon wrote in his magazine articles, was changing its nature. Perhaps it still functioned as an escape apparatus, but it was now going in strongly for propaganda. It was trying to create a false picture of the past years, and a false picture of the Nazis. They had not really been bad guys. Hitler had misled them. What they had been, primarily, were fighters against Communism.

Simon wrote well. He knew his facts. This time his articles had a considerable impact. They led eventually to a best-selling novel by Frederick Forsyth. *The Odessa File* was published internationally, and it featured a whole chapter on Simon Wiesenthal.

But Simon could measure the impact of his articles in another way. The secret men behind ODESSA were furious at his expose of their activities. He began getting letters addressed to *Dirty Jew Wiesenthal*. He got threatening calls at the Documentation Center.

Once he returned home after a speaking engagement to find his wife in a state of collapse, under the care of a doctor. At three A.M. the night before Mrs. Wiesenthal had received an anonymous phone call. It was a woman who said: "Mrs. Wiesenthal, if your husband won't stop raking up the past, my friends are going to get hold of your daughter and you will never see her again."

Simon comforted his wife, and then held his daughter Pauline in his arms a long time. He was shocked and miserable. Should he go on? Could he expose his family to this risk? Was there any sense in continuing the search? No matter how many Nazis he caught, there would be many more left who would go unpunished.

After his wife and child were asleep he argued with himself, but at the end, holding his head in his hands, he could only repeat: "I cannot stop. I cannot stop!"

He did get permission to keep a rifle in his home. Later on, when the family moved from an apartment to a small house, the ground under the lawn was wired so that any intruder coming at night across that lawn would set off an alarm.

Another time he was sitting in his office when a visitor came to the door. Not suspecting anything, his assistant opened the chain and let the man in. The visitor seemed harmless; he wanted to talk to Simon. No sooner was he in the private office than he lunged at Simon with a knife. Simon's reflexes were instantaneous. He threw an inkwell into the man's face, and the man turned and fled, thrusting the assistant out of his way.

He was never caught. Neither Simon nor his helper had seen more than a glimpse of his face and could not identify him.

In spite of these threats, Simon Wiesenthal had to go on. He wrote about the wealth of the SS and asked where had it all gone. The SS had its own Reich Economic Administration. This economic bureau had been responsible for getting the money and property of the Jews, but had not turned it over to the state. It was kept in special SS accounts in banks. Neither the German army nor the German citizens got a penny of it.

For example, a list of what Ernst Kaltenbrunner, SS Gestapo Chief, had accumulated as his share of the loot fell into American hands. Kaltenbrunner was given the death penalty at the Nuremberg trial. Unfortunately, the list was found later so he had not been questioned about it. It included:

50 kilograms of gold bars
50 cases of gold coins and gold articles,
    each case weighing 100 pounds
2,000,000 American dollars
2,000,000 Swiss francs

5 cases filled with diamonds and precious
  stones
1 stamp collection, worth at least 5,000,000
  marks

This was only a fraction of the accumulated SS wealth. A good deal of it had undoubtedly been deposited in other countries, still, in the last weeks of the war there would not have been time to get it all to foreign banks or convert gold bars into cash. Simon had heard rumors, and he advised the Allies to investigate lakes, particularly Toplitzee.

Many years later, in 1959, Simon was proved right. The German magazine *Stern* got permission from the government to conduct an underwater exploration. Fifteen boxes were recovered from Toplitzee. In them was a fortune in counterfeit Bank of England banknotes.

Simon's articles caused consternation in Germany. It was one thing to forgive the SS for their activities under Hitler; it was quite another thing to forgive them for robbing the Jews, and then keeping that wealth from the German people. In the last years of the war civilians and army people had all suffered from lack of money, lack of food. They had had to tighten their belts while the SS had enriched only themselves.

A very hard blow had been struck at the SS prestige. In Germany the former Nazis began to speak and act much more cautiously.

This was not so true of Austrians. Wiesenthal frequently visited the Altaussee region (which was no longer under British control) and he could feel and see the hostility against him. Long before he arrived word that he was coming sped from traffic police to innkeepers to taxi drivers and to every villager.

As he would stroll down the village streets he could hear

the mutters. "It's that Jew Wiesenthal!" "It's that trouble-maker!" "It's that Eichmann-Wiesenthal!" His name was linked in their minds with Eichmann. They all knew he was keeping an eye on the house of Eichmann's ex-wife.

He was not fearsome to look at: medium tall and putting on a little weight, pleasant-faced. It was his eyes they could not meet. Those eyes seemed to strip them of all their pretense of the image they wanted the world to believe of Austrians—jolly, friendly, hard-working, decent, religious people who never hated anyone, especially Jews. He seemed to look into their souls and remind them of things they would rather forget.

Of course, there were some who *were* decent, and who felt ashamed that so many Austrians had become SS men; they would talk to Simon. In 1951 he met a man who had once been a member of the Army counter-intelligence group, who told him he had definite information that Adolf Eichmann was somewhere in South America. Just where, he didn't know.

In the spring of 1952 other friendly people notified Wiesenthal that Frau Liebl (Eichmann's ex-wife) and her three sons had disappeared from Altaussee overnight. The furniture was still in the house and the rent was being paid, but the boys had not gone back to school after the Easter vacation. The family had vanished.

Wiesenthal immediately notified the American and Austrian authorities, but there was little they could do. Frau Liebl was divorced from Eichmann, and on the surface she had lived a blameless life away from him for seven years. No one could accuse her of her husband's crimes. No one could swear she was in touch with him. Not one letter had come to her, directly, from South America.

Yet Wiesenthal knew she was going to Eichmann. The

whole divorce had been a humbug. She was still Eichmann's wife, in spite of the divorce.

Neighbors finally admitted they knew she had obtained German passports from the German consulate in Graz, Austria. Some thought she might have gone to Germany to live with her mother. Simon Wiesenthal was convinced Frau Liebl had spread that rumor as a clever cover-up story; he was certain that, from Germany, she was on her way to South America. But no one in authority had the time nor the excuse to hunt for her. It seemed that she would be able to vanish as securely as her husband.

At this point, when it seemed to Wiesenthal that the Eichmanns had forever escaped him, chance took a hand. As a matter of fact, he found that in most of his investigations a chance remark or a chance meeting led him to unexpected discoveries.

Through his interest in stamp collecting he had met an Austrian baron, who was an enthusiastic collector. The baron invited him to visit his villa, and the two men spent a pleasant evening talking and examining stamps. Then they spoke of Simon Wiesenthal's work. The baron heartily approved of it; he had always hated the Nazis.

The baron also told him he had many friends who felt as he did. In fact, one of his friends had gone to Argentina and had written to the baron about his disgust at finding so many former SS men living there.

"He just sent me this letter," said the baron, handing the envelope to Wiesenthal so he could examine the stamp. "Listen to what he says," and the baron read the letter aloud:

"There are some people here we both used to know. You remember Lieutenant Hoffman from my regiment, and Hauptmann Berger. . . . Imagine whom else I saw—and even had to talk to twice: this awful swine Eichmann who commanded the Jews. He lives near Buenos Aires and works for a water company."

Simon was gripped by excitement. He took the letter and memorized every word of it before handing it back. So now he knew: Eichmann was in Argentina, working for a water company near Buenos Aires.

But with this final knowledge Simon Wiesenthal felt he had done everything he possibly could. He informed the Austrian, German, and American governments. It was up to them to request of Argentina that Eichmann be extradited back to Germany to stand his trial.

Even if the request were made, it was highly unlikely that Argentina would agree to it. They had not deported other Nazis. So Simon Wiesenthal carefully compiled all his notes, his proof of Eichmann's crimes, his long pursuit, and Eichmann's present whereabouts, and made two copies of this investigation. One copy he sent to the World Jewish Congress in New York, and the other he gave to the Israeli consulate. He kept his original notes and photographs.

Five years went by. Israel was too fully occupied during that time in getting the refugees settled, and in building up the economy of the country and its military defense, to pay more than scant attention to the Eichmann files Simon Wiesenthal had sent. But the Israelis had not forgotten Eichmann.

In 1959 the Israelis felt their own state was secure enough to brave the opinion of the world and get Eichmann out of Argentina. It would have to be an illegal operation since Argentina would not deport him voluntarily.

The Wiesenthal files were studied carefully. Then two young men from Israel came to Vienna and asked Simon if he could get them even more up-to-date information. They needed to know the name Eichmann was using in Buenos Aires in order to find him.

Simon Wiesenthal had been busy those past five years with other cases of wanted men, but he put everything aside for the moment and began hunting again through all his Eichmann sources. He visited the baron's villa, hoping there were more letters from his friends in Argentina. But the baron was dead.

Where else could he go? Altaussee yielded nothing; none of the ex-wife's neighbors had heard from her. So Wiesenthal sent one of his helpers to Czechoslovakia to interview Frau Maria Liebl, the mother of Eichmann's ex-wife. She was hostile. She said she knew nothing. She said her daughter had nothing whatever to do with Eichmann, but that her daughter had emigrated to Argentina and had now married a man whose name was Klems or Klemt or something like that.

Had she any letters from her daughter? she was asked. No, she replied, and no address for her, either.

The helper came back from Czechoslovakia a discouraged man. But Simon was elated. Without realizing it, the mother had given them valuable information.

First, Frau Liebl had remarried. Second, the husband's name was something like Klemt. Simon was absolutely convinced that Frau Liebl had remarried Eichmann under this new name he had taken.

Simon passed the information to the Israelis and told them to check the marriage records in Argentina. They did, and notified Simon that the ex-Mrs. Eichmann had indeed married in Buenos Aires. Her new husband was a Ricardo Klement who worked for a water company. But they could not be absolutely certain that the Ricardo Klement they were now watching day and night was actually Adolf Eichmann. Klement was older than the pictures of the young Eichmann that Simon Wiesenthal had given them. He did not resemble very closely the pictures of the arrogant, uniformed SS man. Could Wiesenthal give them something more recent?

He understood their caution. They had said nothing to him of their plans, but he knew. He knew they were going to smuggle Eichmann out of Argentina. It would be a disaster, an international scandal, if they got the wrong man.

Simon had a sudden idea. Eichmann had brothers still living in Linz, and all the Eichmann men looked very much alike. The Eichmann father had just died and the funeral date had been announced in the newspapers. So Simon Wiesenthal hired two excellent photographers and told them to get photos at the grave site of the family without the family knowing the pictures were being taken.

The day of the funeral was dark and cloudy. Simon worried. The photographers must shoot from a considerable distance away, and from behind shrubbery. Could they possibly get a distinct picture from that distance and in such poor light? Nor could he be sure his idea would provide the evidence he wanted. The brothers might not look as much alike now as when they were younger.

Then the photographers returned with their developed prints, and Simon's spirits soared. The pictures were sharp and clear. The faces of Emil and Otto and Friedrich and Robert Eichmann, the brothers, were plainly visible—and they still resembled each other remarkably. They were middle-aged men, now, but so was the other Eichmann. It was very likely that he, too, had kept those special family features.

It was clear to Wiesenthal now why Adolf had been reported as being seen here and there in Austria while he was actually in Argentina. People had mistaken his brothers for him.

The photographers had taken group shots and also individual shots of each brother. Moving the pictures around on his table and comparing each one with the young photograph of Adolf Eichmann, Simon decided that brother Otto most closely resembled Adolf.

Simon had the Israelis study the photographs carefully and patiently, noting the shape of the heads, the chins, the eyes, and the mouths. There were slight differences, of course, but the Eichmann face was there in all of them, particularly in Otto's.

Elated, the Israelis took all the snapshots with them. They told Herr Wiesenthal, with thanks, that they might well be the proof they needed.

On May 23, 1960, newspapers all over the world carried the headline news that Adolf Eichmann was in a prison in Jerusalem where he would be held for trial. He had been captured, questioned (he admitted his real identity), then drugged and smuggled from Argentina on a plane.

Now it was possible for the Israelis to tell Simon how directly responsible he had been for that capture. He had led them to Ricardo Klements and then had provided them with the photographs that clinched the identification.

One small additional proof had been provided by Eichmann himself. He had made a slip the Israelis learned of. He had brought flowers to his wife to celebrate their wedding anniversary, but the date on which he had brought the flowers was *not* that of the marriage between Klement and Frau Liebl, but the marriage date of Eichmann and Frau Liebl many years before.

The long, long search and the patient detective work was over. Simon Wiesenthal went to Jerusalem for the trial and saw for the first time the man he had pursued so long.

Newspapermen were there from all over the world. Many knew or had heard of Simon Wiesenthal. They wanted to interview him. He shook them off; his job was over. "This is quite a triumph for you, isn't it, Mr. Wiesenthal?" said one.

Simon shook his head. He left the courtroom, which was now tense with emotion as witness after witness described the horrors of the death camps Eichmann had organized. Simon walked to the mausoleum of Yad Vashem, the memorial to the six million Jews who had perished in the Holocaust. He went in through the bronze doors and walked through the Hall of Remembrance and stood at the railing looking down at the Eternal Flame. Written there were the names of the death camps: Maidenek and Sobibor and Belsen and Treblinka and Buchenwald and Mauthausen, and all the others.

Now, he thought, perhaps the dead can sleep more quietly.

Chapter Seven

The trial came at just the right moment in history. It acted like a shock wave, especially in Germany. During the past years the crimes of the SS seemed to have been forgotten. Now all these buried crimes were being brought out into the light. The prisoner Eichmann was talking. He was not only admitting to what he had done but to what others had done as well.

There were no protests at the death sentence he received.

If he was guilty, what about the others who had never been brought to trial? Germany seemed to feel it was time to clean house. A new generation of Germans who had never been infected by Hitler's doctrines wanted to know just what had happened and why. Why should the guilty have escaped justice?

There was a new wave of arrests and convictions. There was an enormous increase in the correspondence going in and out of the Documentation Center in Vienna. German prosecutors and judges wanted access to Wiesenthal's files.

This interest in bringing to justice the murderers who had thought themselves safe in Germany did not extend to Austria. In Austria Simon found the same resistance to uncovering the truth as there always had been.

In 1955 the four-power occupation of Austria had come to an end. The country regained her status as a sovereign nation. Almost the first thing the government did was to grant amnesty to many Austrian Nazis whom the occupation forces of the Allies had put in jail. Austria also signed a treaty with the Soviet Union whereby Austrian prisoners-of-war who had been tried and imprisoned in Russia would be returned to Austria. Under the terms of that treaty the returned prisoners were not to go free. They were to serve out the remainder of their sentences, or be tried under Austrian law and get new sentences.

Simon Wiesenthal noted that Franz Murer's name was not on the list that Austria published of the returned prisoners. At the time he thought nothing of it. Evidently the "Butcher of Wilna," whom Simon had found on his chicken farm, was still held by the Soviets. Perhaps he was too big a criminal for them to let out of their hands.

The Murer file, with all the witnesses' affidavits, was still in the Documentation Center, but in the inactive group. Wiesenthal was busy with other cases.

One of them was a man named Rokita.

In 1958 on a train going to Geneva, Switzerland, for a conference, Wiesenthal met a Danish military officer. The two men discovered that they both had been in the same concentration camp of Grossrosen. Simon asked the Dane if he remembered Richard Rokita, the deputy camp commander.

"What did he look like?" asked the Dane.

Simon Wiesenthal described Rokita's broad face, thick, pouting lips, and pig eyes, and mentioned that Rokita played the violin.

The Dane shook his head. Rokita must not have been at Grossrosen when he was there. "But," said he, "it is an odd thing. I recall that after the war, in 1947 or 1948, I happened to be in the Hamburg Officers' Club—an Allied Officers' Club—and a German band was playing there. The violin player looked just like your description of Rokita."

It was probably not the right man, but Simon had learned never to ignore the slightest hint or clue. Rokita would have had to find a job, and outside of beating Jews his only other interest was the violin. He had been a strange, terrifying murderer. He loved to kill his victims to the sound of music. He had forced a Jewish composer to write a "death tango" which was played during executions. The sound of the violin and the sound his pistol made as he shot at Jews were both sweet to his ears. He would smile with happiness as his orchestra blended with dying cries and agonies.

Simon reported the Dane's information to the prosecutor of War Crimes in northern Germany, but a search through the musicians' unions of Hamburg and Lubeck and Bremen revealed no Rokita. However, one musician said he had met a man of Rokita's description, under the name of Domagala.

There was no Domagala listed among the musicians' membership, either. Then Simon had an inspiration. If the violin player were working—either in a band or at some other trade—he would likely have registered for government health insurance. Why not check there?

That night the prosecutor called him. "You were right. There is a man named Domagala in Hamburg and he is registered for health insurance. He used to be a musician, but now he is a night watchman."

Richard Rokita-Domagala was caught. He admitted his identity, his SS record, his crimes. The War Crimes prosecutor took charge of his arrest and trial, and Simon Wiesenthal could close the file on another murderer brought to justice.

From the moment the war had ended Austria had been determined to make the world believe it had been a "conquered" nation, and not a partner with Germany in the war. This was just not true. It *was* true that the German Army had made a mock-invasion of Austria, but the Austrians had lined the streets and cheered and tossed flowers to the Nazis.

Many, many of the SS concentration camp guards and commanders all over Europe had come from Austria. There were Gestapo agents in Holland and Belgium and France and Poland who had come from Austria.

But Austria did not want the world to know this. Austria did not want trials which would expose how deeply it had been committed to Nazi ideas. Austria sheltered and protected its war criminals.

Simon Wiesenthal, working in the heart of Austria, was a thorn in the nation's flesh. Some prominent newspapermen applauded what he was doing, but he ran into opposition from the government, the police, the judges and courts, and from most of the people.

Ordinarily a quiet and reasonable man, Wiesenthal could become an eloquent and passionate speaker, and a driving force when he uncovered a lie and exposed deliberate treachery. He was especially angry that the new, young generation of Austrians were being taught falsehoods.

One October night in 1958, just before he moved his office to Vienna, a friend came to his apartment in Linz and invited Simon to go with him that evening to the stage performance of *The Diary of Anne Frank* at the Landestheater.

Simon had read the *Diary* (or, as it was sometimes named: *Anne Frank, The Diary of a Young Girl*) and had been deeply moved by this account written by an adolescent Jewish girl in Holland under the German conquerors. Anne was only thirteen when the Nazi order was issued that all Jews were to be rounded up and deported.

Her father, Otto Frank, had already made his plans to hide his family. His closest Dutch business friends had helped him turn the attic room of his warehouse into something like a home with a kitchen, bedrooms and a sitting room. Here, on Wednesday, July 8, 1942, came Mr. and Mrs. Frank, their older daughter Margot, thirteen-year-old Anne. Later another couple, the Van Daans and their son, Peter, and another man, a dentist, joined them.

The attic rooms became crowded. The group had to be extremely quiet during the day when there were workers below in the warehouse. They could only move about and speak freely, and cook and do household duties at night. Life was difficult, but Anne could endure it. What she missed most was a girl friend to talk to, so she began her diary and talked to it, pouring out all her problems, her small joys, her fears.

The family lived hidden for more than two years. They were betrayed and captured in August of 1944. They were all sent to concentration camps, and Anne died of typhus at Belsen.

Of all of them, only Otto Frank, the father, survived. After the war he came back to Amsterdam where he met the business friends who had so faithfully helped him during the years of hiding. They told him that the Gestapo had inquired if there were any jewels in the attic; when they saw that there were none they had contemptuously scattered all the papers they found onto the floor. Among the papers was Anne's diary. The friends had rescued it and now they gave it to Otto. After several years more, when the wounds in his heart were no longer so fresh, Otto Frank allowed it to be published.

It had proved to be a sensation and was translated all over the world, made into a movie, and adapted for the stage. So Simon was eager to see this performance in Austria.

But even before the curtain went up there was a wild disturbance in the theater. Groups of very young demonstrators in the balcony shouted: "Traitors! Toadies! Swindlers!" They booed the actors when the show started, and made such a noise the performance stopped and the theater house lights came on. Now a shower of leaflets were flung down from the balcony.

Simon picked one up and read it. It said: "This play is a fraud. Anne Frank never existed. The Jews have invented the whole story because they want to extort more restitution money. Don't believe a word of it! It's a fake!"

Police arrived and took down the names of some of the demonstrators who were students of Linz high schools. The lights dimmed again and the performance went on. When the play ended Simon walked out to find police cars all around, but the students were still out in force in the streets, handing out leaflets, shouting, and arguing.

Simon went from group to group, just listening and saying nothing. What he heard shocked him. They honestly did believe the *Diary* was a fake. There was no Anne Frank. It was all a fiction story written by someone else to enlist sympathy for the Jews.

He knew the story was true, but he could also understand why these young people believed it was false. The *Diary* was not the usual kind of a diary that most people kept. Anne had been desperately lonely for a girl friend she could talk to and reveal her innermost feelings so she had invented a friend and called her "Kitty." And each day in her diary she wrote to Kitty as to another person, telling her little details of her life but also telling her of her studies, her occasional naughtiness, her arguments with her mother, her dislike of young Peter Van Daan and, finally the growth of her shy and tender and bewildered love for Peter.

Not only was the diary an unusual one but so was Anne's talent for writing and expressing herself. The concentration camp not only killed a young girl, but also destroyed what might have become a brilliant writing career.

However, most young people all over the world had no doubts that she had written the book. They loved the story and loved Anne Frank. Only in Austria—and perhaps parts of Germany—was there this angry disbelief. Simon knew it was mainly because the Austrian parents had already told their children that the Jews were liars and the Nazis had not been bad people.

The demonstrating students had been babies when Anne Frank had been arrested. As they grew up they wanted to be proud of Austria, so it was easy for them to believe their parents and teachers who fed them lies.

How could he, Simon Wiesenthal, convince them of the truth? He had to give them facts. They thought they were right. They were scornful of the young people from other nations who came to Europe and made pilgrimages to Anne Frank's grave.

He talked to a priest in Vienna who told him that his students absolutely refused to believe in the atrocities of concentration camps, even of Mauthausen which had been in Austria. His students had argued with him, saying, yes, there had been detention camps for Jews but the gas chambers were only used to disinfect their clothes because Jews were so dirty.

Two days after the theater demonstration Simon was in a coffee house with a friend, talking about it. The friend saw a group of high school students at another table. He called one of the boys over. "Were you at the demonstration?" he asked.

"No, I'm sorry I wasn't. But," the boy added proudly, "my friends were."

"And you think the *Diary* is a fake?"

"Of course," the boy answered. "There's absolutely no evidence that Anne Frank ever lived, ever stayed in that attic, was arrested or died in a concentration camp." The boy went on to say that Otto Frank could have written it himself, or someone else must have. It was a clever forgery, the student insisted.

Simon listened. This boy was not bad or mean or a deliberate liar. He honestly believed what he was saying. He had to be given proof. Simon spoke up: "Young man, if we could prove to you that Anne Frank existed, would you accept the diary as genuine?"

"How could *you* prove it?" The student was just humoring Wiesenthal.

"Suppose the Gestapo officer who actually arrested Anne Frank were found. Suppose he admitted it—would you and your friends accept that as proof?"

The student looked startled and confused. He was convinced there was no Gestapo officer. "Yes," said the boy, "if you can find him, and the man admits it."

It was a gigantic job Simon Wiesenthal had set himself: to find a man who had made an arrest in Holland fourteen years ago, and a man who was probably just a minor SS official.

Gestapo men were sometimes moved from place to place. This particular one might have ended the war in a completely different part of Europe. He might have been investigated, found guilty of minor crimes, served a small sentence and been released to go—where? He might even be dead.

Anne's father, Otto Frank, was contacted but he did not know the name of the Gestapo leader, nor did Mr. Frank want to cooperate with any investigation. He had allowed the *Diary* to be published. That was enough. His own pain and anguish ran too deeply for him to want to recall the past.

Then Wiesenthal found, in one version of the book, an appendix written by Paul Kraler, who had been one of the Dutch friends who had supplied the people in the attic with food and books and other necessities. Kraler wrote that, after the Franks and the others were arrested, he had gone to Gestapo headquarters to see if he could do anything to save them. At headquarters he had talked with the arresting officer.

The man, he wrote, was called Silvernagl and he was an *Austrian!* He was Viennese.

It seemed to be a wonderful clue. Much excited, Simon Wiesenthal went to Vienna and started tracing. It could be Silvernagl, but it could also be Silbernagl, which was a common Austrian name. Mr. Kraler had only heard the name spoken, not written, and he could have misunderstood.

Wiesenthal worked carefully through the Viennese phone books, checking on every possible Silvernagl-Silbernagl. He went to every government agency; he asked banks to check their records. He even hired a detective agency to help him.

He turned up absolutely nothing. Not one of the Silvernagls or Silbernagls interviewed, nor any of their relatives, revealed the slightest trace of any connection with an SS man who had served in Gestapo headquarters in Holland at any time. It was a dead end.

Still Wiesenthal could not and would not give up. When friends said he was wasting his time for nothing, he answered that it was not for nothing—it was for all the youth of Austria. He had promised to give them proof.

He was invited to appear on a Dutch television program to speak of his work. He made useful contacts during that time, and on his next visit to Amsterdam he talked over the dilemma he was facing trying to prove Anne Frank had really lived in that attic. Two of his new Dutch friends with whom he talked were Ben A. Sijes of the Dutch Institute for War Documentation, and Mr. Taconis, a Dutch police official. Of course, they were not only interested in Anne Frank. They were still pursuing SS criminals who had operated in Holland, and so they talked with Wiesenthal about many other unsolved problems.

As Simon Wiesenthal was about to leave to catch his plane back to Austria, Mr. Taconis arrived and handed him some "travel literature" for him to read during his flight home. The "literature" turned out to be a photostatic copy of the wartime 1943 telephone directory of the Gestapo in Holland, with about three hundred names in it.

Once Simon was settled into his airplane seat and the flight took off, he leafed through the pages, running his eyes down the lists of names, from every city and town in Holland. Names. Names. Some he recognized from War Crimes trials; most he did not. He was getting sleepy and was almost dozing off when he turned a page and saw that it was headed Section IV, Sonderkommando, and underneath was a subheading Section IV B *Joden* (Jews). He came alert. Section IV B referred to Eichmann's organization. The Gestapo had other functions. Their job was to arrest anyone causing trouble for Hitler's Reich, but Section IV dealt with the Jews.

Under Amsterdam there were four names listed: Kempin —Buschmann—Scherf—Silberbauer.

Silberbauer. Could it be possible that Paul Kraler, emotionally overwrought, pleading at Gestapo headquarters, had thought he heard Silvernagl when actually he had heard *Silberbauer?* It was possible. Probably both the Dutchman and the Austrian spoke German, but an Austrian-German accent would be strange to a Hollander like Paul Kraler.

And Section IV would certainly be the group responsible for arresting Jews such as the Franks.

Simon Wiesenthal was no longer sleepy. He was anxious for the plane to land in Vienna. No sooner did he reach home than he reached for the telephone book. Yes, there were twelve Silberbauers listed. It *was* an Austrian name.

From experience, Wiesenthal knew that all twelve might resist talking to him, be evasive or be hostile to him. Or he might alarm the one he wanted and give him a chance to get away. The investigation of names before had been long and wearying, and Wiesenthal did not want to ask the same people for help again.

He sat down to think.

What sort of work would a man like Silberbauer very likely take up after the war? What was he fitted for? He had been trained in the SS Gestapo for police woik. Might it not be possible that he would come home to Vienna and try to get an ordinary police job after the war? He had not been connected with brutalities at concentration camps. He was unimportant. The Allied War Crimes departments would have paid no attention to him, and certainly Austria would not have cared whatever he had done.

That this Silberbauer might go into peacetime police work was no wild guess. Already Wiesenthal had found that many ex-SS men, with no other training or skill, just naturally had wound up in city, state, or national police forces.

Anyway, it was worth a try. He called up Dr. Josef Wiesinger, head of the proper department of the Austrian Ministry of the Interior which dealt with police forces, and also with investigation of Nazi crimes.

Simon told Dr. Josef Wiesinger that he had found the man who had arrested Anne Frank; that his name was Silberbauer; and that he was now a Viennese policeman. This was rash and reckless, but Simon knew very well that important men in the Ministry of the Interior were busy men who did not like to be bothered with just guesswork.

Dr. Wiesinger took his word for it, but protested that Silberbauer was such a common name there must be at least six on the Viennese police force. What was the first name?

Simon Wiesenthal did not know. He suggested it should not be difficult to find out. All that was necessary was to go into the records of all six and find out which one was with the Gestapo Section IV in Amsterdam in August of 1944.

The next day he sent in the usual written request for the information, to Dr. Wiesinger's office.

He got no answer. Day after day he telephoned or went to the office and always he got the same runaround. The files, he was told, were "being examined." He knew this was nonsense. How long did it take to examine the records of five or six Silberbauers in the police files?

To Simon's astonishment, the newspaper of the Austrian Communist Party came out on November 11 with a headline story that Police Inspector Karl Silberbauer of the Viennese police force had been suspended from his duties. He was suspected of being involved in the arrest of Anne Frank while he was a Gestapo officer in Holland.

Simon Wiesenthal was not only astonished, he was angry. He had made a promise to the youth of Austria that he would reveal the truth to them. Now it would seem as if the Communists had uncovered it.

He called Dr. Wiesinger, who was most embarrassed. The long delay had been because the police chiefs were so humiliated at the knowledge that they had not only hired an SS man but had made him an Inspector that they had stalled and stalled. They thought they could just suspend Silberbauer and keep it quiet. Then Silberbauer himself had talked. Someone had overheard him and given the news to the Communist newspaper.

Simon promptly called a news conference of *all* Austrian and foreign reporters and told them the actual details of how the man had been traced. He could also tell the reporters that Karl Silberbauer had admitted that he was in charge of the Gestapo group who had gone to the Amsterdam attic and arrested the Franks and the others. He remembered young Anne very well.

The news conference did everything Simon hoped for, and more. There were headlines in newspapers all over Austria, all over Europe. Austrian youth could no longer call her *Diary* a fake. Perhaps from now on they would begin to sort out truth from lies, and accept Austria's guilt.

He did not seek to have Silberbauer punished any further. The exposure, and perhaps the man's own conscience, were punishment enough.

What was important was that, once again, Simon Wiesenthal had kept faith with the dead. The ghost of the lovely, bright young girl, murdered in her teens, could be at rest. Anne Frank had been vindicated.

Chapter Eight

All during 1959 and 1960 Simon Wiesenthal was following Eichmann, but there were other cases to attend to as well. He was tracing a man named Erich Rajakowitsch, who had been Eichmann's chief deputy in Holland. Rajakowitsch was responsible for rounding up of all Dutch Jews for deportation to death camps, and for rounding up other Hollanders for forced labor in Germany. He was by citizenship a Viennese, and by training a lawyer.

Everyone seemed to assume he had died in the last days of the war, but Simon Wiesenthal did not believe so. He forced the Austrian authorities to issue a warrant for Rajakowitsch's arrest. This kept the file on him officially open, instead of being closed as "presumed dead."

Then Wiesenthal began visiting countless numbers of Rajakowitsch's old acquaintances in Vienna. As so often happened with Wiesenthal's patient investigations, he listened to a word dropped here, a word there, watched a smile on a man's face as the man told an obvious lie, and finally someone blurted out the truth.

Rajakowitsch had survived the war. He had been for a while in an American prisoner-of-war camp, had escaped, lived hidden for a while in Austria and then moved to Trieste, Italy.

The Trieste clue was an important one because Wiesenthal already knew that Rajakowitsch had been born in Trieste, and he would very likely have relatives and friends there who would help him—and might also, unwillingly, help Wiesenthal.

He wanted to follow up this clue but it was now 1960 and Eichmann's trial was on. The Documentation Center was frantically busy gathering up as much new material as they could to help the prosecutor's case in the trial. Simon Wiesenthal especially needed some information on Franz Murer, the Butcher of Wilna, who had been part of Eichmann's network as commander of Wilna. He wanted to show the direct link between the two men.

Of course Murer was in a Soviet Union prison. He had not been returned to Austria, Simon thought, when the other war crimes prisoners had been sent back under the Austrian–Soviet treaty. So Wiesenthal telephoned the police post nearest the Austrian chicken farm where Murer had been arrested back in 1947. He asked the police if they knew where any of Murer's letters and documents were.

Their answer shocked him. "Why don't you ask Murer himself?" they asked.

"Isn't he dead? Or in a Soviet prison?" Simon asked.

"Not at all. He came back four years ago and he's lived on his farm here ever since," came the reply.

Four years ago! Then Murer *had* been returned by the Soviets under the Austrian treaty. Why was his name not on the list of Austrians published? Why had he not been tried again by Austrian courts? Why was he free?

Simon Wiesenthal was sure he knew why, but at least he could try to force the authorities to admit what they had done. He wrote, he called upon Ministers, he went to the

War Crimes office—and ran into a blank wall of silence. No one would speak to him of Murer. When he demanded to know why Franz Murer, one of the most bloodthirsty of all the SS men, was now back living in prosperity on his farm (so highly respected in his community that he had been elected chairman of the District Agricultural Chamber), all he got from one man was a shrug of the shoulders. One man did speak: he said that, after all, Murer had spent some time in a Soviet jail, and, anyway, why should Austrians be concerned with what Murer did so far away in Wilna, to a bunch of Latvians and Jews?

Simon wrote formally to the Austrian Ministry of Justice asking for an explanation and for action. The Ministry replied that, if Mr. Wiesenthal had any evidence against Mr. Franz Murer, it should be supplied in writing to Section Eleven of the Ministry.

He submitted the affidavits of murder and brutality which were in his files. He was told they were worthless. They were old. They had been used in the 1947 trial. Mr. Wiesenthal would have to get fresh evidence and live witnesses if he hoped to get Murer arrested for a new trial.

Simon faced the official who told him this, and tried to make him understand the deeper meanings of crime and punishment. "Human life," he said, "is too short to expiate the crimes Murer committed in Wilna. I am not looking for vengeance—only justice. Murer was sentenced to twenty-five years. He only served a few. According to the terms of the State Treaty with the Soviet Union he should have again been tried before an Austrian court."

The official was weary of the discussion. He just repeated that if Mr. Wiesenthal could find new evidence then the Ministry would have to take action.

Simon walked out of the office into the street. He knew the Ministry neither expected he would find new evidence nor even wanted him to. If there were to be a new trial of Murer it was going to be twice as difficult as before. The witnesses were scattered all over the globe. The government of Austria would be hostile: there was an election to be held soon, and there were over fifty million ex-Nazi Party members in Austria who could vote. No one in the government or in the courts wanted to antagonize those voters.

Simon walked slowly through the streets of Vienna. This was one of the most beautiful cities in the world. It was a jewel of cities. As an architect, Simon Wiesenthal appreciated the beauty of its great palaces, its medieval guildhalls, St. Stephen's Cathedral, and the Opera House. Aside from its physical grandeur, Vienna had always been renowned for its music and gaiety, its Strauss waltzes, its coffee houses where the Viennese met to gossip and read newspapers.

Simon passed the Opera building and came to the famous Sacher's hotel and restaurant, and he smiled as he thought of the wonderful food in there, especially the cake called the Sacher torte. It seemed to typify the way the Viennese liked to think of themselves—a superabundance of good, rich living.

Then he stopped smiling. On the surface Vienna was busy restoring her old image. Tourists were being put up in fine hotels and waited upon with old-fashioned courtesy and proudly shown, with old-fashioned hospitality, the famous sights of the city. Tourists drank wine with the Viennese and heard them singing.

But they did not hear, as Simon Wiesenthal did, the sound of Nazi jackboots in the streets and the coarse singing of the Nazi *Horst Wessel* song, the marching and the demonstrations when the Austrian Nazis yelled in unison: "Austria, arise—Jews perish!"

He felt that the clean smiles and gaiety of the city were false. Underneath the wholesomeness was a poison. The Austrians did not want to remember what they had done, but until they did admit their guilt the poison would go on festering. It needed to be uncovered and then drained away.

Pretending that Franz Murer was just a good fellow, a good farmer and a good neighbor was such a monstrous deception! For Austria's own sake, and particularly for the sake of the young generation, he must be exposed for what he really was.

When he climbed the stairs in the shabby building where the Documentation Center was housed, Simon Wiesenthal was already turning over in his head all the witnesses who had signed affidavits before him testifying to Murer's incredible brutalities. He would have to get more witnesses and bring them to Vienna, if possible. He must get new evidence before the courts.

He wrote letters to every witness in his files; he wrote to Jewish agencies in America and he wrote to Israel, asking for cooperation from any person who had lived in Wilna during Murer's time.

The response was amazing. Right after the war Wiesenthal had had difficulty getting stories from people because they were so shocked by recent memories that they would become hysterical, burst into tears and run from him. Some refused to talk at all. Now that so many years had elapsed these same people had become healed, in a measure, and they could let themselves remember.

It was as unthinkable to them, as to Wiesenthal, that Franz Murer should escape so lightly. When their letters and affidavits came to the Documentation Center, Simon Wiesenthal could well understand their feelings.

One affidavit was from a Wolf Fainberg, now living in New Jersey. He wrote about an incident in December, 1941, when Murer had stopped him at the ghetto entrance to ask for his work pass. While Fainberg was looking for it, a little,

ten-year-old, hunchbacked child went by. Murer said to his
assistant: "Look at the misfits you are keeping in this ghetto,"
and pulled out his revolver and shot the child dead.

Another man, Isak Kulkin, sent his sworn testimony from
California. He had witnessed the hanging of six Jews. The
rope had broken for one, and that one knelt before Murer,
begging that his life be spared. Murer simply ordered him
to be strung up again on a stronger rope.

Another man wrote of a day of horror so terrible it seemed
unbelievable.

Murer—the Butcher of Wilna—had had enough of small
children and babies who interfered with their mothers' abil-
ity to slave for him. He ordered all mothers with small children to assemble in the square of the labor camp. Once
there, mothers and children were separated. The screams of
the frightened babies and the pleas and cries of the mothers
bothered Murer not at all. If a mother fought to keep her
child it was torn from her.

The affidavit read:

"Babies were thrown through the air like parcels. Heart-
rending scenes took place, but Murer remained inflexible.
One woman clasped her child to her chest and fought the
SS men. They threw the mother and the child on the truck.
She was a pharmacist who had studied in Berlin. She cried
'Is this German civilization?' Murer ordered her taken off
the truck and told his adjutant, Martin Weiss, to shoot her
right away. Her body was left hanging on the barbed-wire
fence."

The children were all loaded onto the trucks and driven
away, and everyone knew it was for their mass death and
mass grave. Now the women, without their children, could
give Murer more working time.

All these were new stories, but Wiesenthal wanted to get
some of the old ones used at the former trial. Affidavits would

not be enough; he had to produce the witnesses themselves, who might remember new details. He got in touch with them and a few agreed to come to Vienna.

The mass of testimony Wiesenthal accumulated did not stir the Ministry into any kind of action. They ignored his request for the trial, so the Jewish Congregation in Vienna called a press conference. Simon Wiesenthal spoke. He gave the Austrian and foreign newspapermen and magazine representatives the full story of Franz Murer.

There was shock and anger. The press were furious that the infamous Butcher of Wilna should be living the tranquil life of a farmer in Austria. The Eichmann trial was still going on, and Murer's name had cropped up frequently. He was not some unknown, minor SS man. The newspaper stories and editorials demanded that Austria bring Murer to trial.

Finally the government gave in. Murer was arrested and put on trial in the city of Graz on June 10, 1963. He was charged with seventeen counts of "murder by his own hand."

A good many witnesses paid their own way to come to the trial in person, even from the United States. One of these was Jacob Brodi, who had seen Murer shoot his seventeen-year-old son Daniel right in front of him. The father had brooded over this tragedy for all these years. He arrived from the United States with a knife and a fixed determination to go into the courtroom, walk up to Murer, and kill the assassin of his son. He wanted to kill him with his own hands, as Murer had killed Daniel.

Simon talked him out of this vengeance. They must not become murderers like the Nazis. Let the law punish Murer. Brodi's hands must not be stained with his blood.

Brodi was hard to convince. "Words, Mr. Wiesenthal, nothing but words. Your child was not murdered. My boy was murdered."

What had Simon been doing all these years since the war but demanding justice for all the children who had been murdered? "I still cry sometimes, Mr. Brodi," he said, "when I hear what happened to children in the concentration camps. I did cry when I heard about your boy. Because he could have been mine. Your child was also my child. Do you really believe I could go on with my work if I didn't feel that way?"

Then Jacob Brodi broke into hard, wrenching sobs, and slowly handed over his knife to Simon.

From the moment the trial opened, Simon wondered if he had done the right thing. The atmosphere in the courtroom was solidly sympathetic to Franz Murer; hostile and jeering to the Jewish witnesses. The courtroom audience smiled at Murer, broke into handclapping whenever his defense lawyer spoke, was openly scornful of even the deep emotion of Daniel Brodi's story. Franz Murer turned around frequently and smiled and waved at friends. They might as well have been at a picnic.

No matter how much terrible evidence Simon Wiesenthal produced, the cards were stacked in favor of Franz Murer. The judge, the jury, and the audience were on the side of their "good" Austrian against those foreign Jews. All Franz Murer had to say was that people such as Brodi were mistaken; that it was a pity his son was killed, but someone else must have done it. Murer was believed.

He was acquitted to wild cheering.

Simon Wiesenthal could hardly face Jacob Brodi. He had promised the man justice. He had stopped him from his personal vengeance. Now Brodi must go home, embittered, while his child's murderer was free and cheered and applauded.

Bitter himself, Simon walked out of the courtroom to the Vienna streets—and saw a very strange sight.

Massed in front of the court building and marching slowly down the street was a great crowd of Catholic youth, shouting out: "Murer is a murderer! Murer must be punished!" Simon's heart lifted with the uplifted banners they carried, proclaiming their outrage against the verdict.

He stood and watched. The trial, then, had not been a failure. It was never vengeance he sought, but that the people be awakened to the truth and be on guard that never again could the Nazi ideology flourish again to nurture beasts like Murer.

That night there was a special service of penitence in the Catholic church of Michaeler to express the remorse of the decent Viennese for the crimes that Christians had done to the Jews. As Austria is a Catholic country, this was a most significant action.

In addition, Austrian and international newspapers covering the trial were vehement in their disgust and fury at Murer's acquittal. They proclaimed that Austrian justice—judge and jury—were a shame to the nation.

Simon Wiesenthal could believe that attitudes were changing in Austria. He had done his part to change them. He would go on doing it.

Now he had time to consider Rajakowitsch, in the Italian city of Trieste. Information had been coming into the Documentation Center. Patiently Simon and his volunteer sifted all information from the letters about Rajakowitsch, and they found that he had, indeed, gone to Trieste after the war. He must have taken with him a large fortune in Nazi loot (or been helped by ODESSA) because he had invested a big sum of money in the import-export firm called Enneri & Co.

It also seemed likely that Rajakowitsch was more than just an investor in the company. He might be a silent partner, because the cable address of Enneri & Co. was RAJARICO.

The Documentation Center had some friends in Italy and it was not too difficult a job for them to investigate Enneri & Co. They found that the headquarters of the business had been shifted from Trieste to Milan, and that the man who was now in full control of the firm was a man called Raja. And Signor Raja was living openly in Milan, a most prosperous, respected businessman!

Even though Simon Wiesenthal was certain Raja and Rajakowitsch were the same person, he found himself again hampered by the Austrian authorities. Very quietly they had dropped the warrant for Rajakowitsch's arrest, for "lack of evidence," even though Wiesenthal had submitted to them proof that he had not only been Eichmann's man in Holland, he had first been Eichmann's man in Austria and responsible for the deportation of Austrian Jews.

Once again the Austrian Ministry demanded *new* evidence for a new warrant to be issued.

This time it was easy. The Dutch State Institute of War Documentation in Amsterdam, Holland, was only too happy to supply Simon with a full acount of Rajakowitsch's activities in searching out Dutch Jews and transporting them to concentration camps. By March of 1962, Wiesenthal had a great wealth of material to submit to the Austrian Ministry—which they could not ignore without offending Holland.

Then he went to Milan and conferred with police authorities there. They were amazed. How had he ever discovered that a supposedly dead Austrian Nazi was a much-alive Milanese businessman? How many secret agents did Wiesenthal have working for him in Italy?

Wiesenthal thought this very funny. They were thinking in terms of a great network of secret agents. True, he did have a few friends here and there who would answer his questions in letters, but almost all the work of tracing Raja had been done behind his desk at the Document Center. First, the clue that Trieste had been the man's birthplace; the guess there might be relatives; another guess that he would either have resumed his legal practice or gone into business; the discovery of his connection with the firm that had RAJARICO as its cable address. The rest had been easy.

The idea that the Documentation Center was the headquarters of a great spy organization was a long way from the simple truth.

The Italian police wanted very much to help him nab Raja, but Raja had committed no crime in Italy. The Austrian Ambassador to Italy would have to formally request the Italians to arrest him and return him to Austria, as an Austrian citizen wanted for crimes committed there.

The Austrian Ambassador took his orders from the Foreign Ministry in Vienna, so back to Vienna went Simon. There he ran into the usual stalling. He was sent from one department to another. "Extradite Erich Raja from Italy? How do we know he is Rajakowitsch? Where is your proof?" he was asked.

Ordinarily a very self-controlled man, Simon Wiesenthal could become extremely forceful in words and movements when he was aroused. He told them in no uncertain terms what he thought of their questions and their delaying tactics.

They were shamed by his vehemence, but they came up with another stall. Unfortunately, the attorney general was going away on his vacation and the matter would have to wait until he returned.

The matter could not wait. At any moment Raja might get a tip—even from some of the Viennese people Simon had talked to—and he could vanish on a plane to South America.

Simon decided on a bold and risky step. Breaking the case wide open would certainly tell Raja he had been discovered. Yet the publicity, and the widest, noisiest publicity, might embarrass the Austrians into action, and it would enable the Italian police to guard airports and keep Raja from getting away.

Simon went back to Milan. He called on the Vienna correspondent of the biggest Italian newspaper, which was read all over Italy and all over Europe. On April 8 he gave him the story. Two hours after the interview the newspaper *Corriere Della Sera*—without Simon's knowledge—sent a reporter to the home of Raja to check out the facts. Raja's son said his father was busy; he would come to the newspaper office in the morning.

He never did. Instead, he went to his bank and drew out a huge sum of money, got into his red Fiat automobile and drove away. Again he had disappeared.

When Simon Wiesenthal heard this he felt he had made a great mistake in talking to the newspaper. The editor was also sorry and admitted he should never have sent a reporter to alert Raja.

However, the mistake turned out to be nothing of the kind. By that same day the story of Raja-Rajakowitsch was a headline not only in Italy, but in newspapers all over Europe. Raja was a marked man and so was his red Fiat. His picture was published. The license plate on his car was published.

It was quickly reported that he had crossed the Italian border into Switzerland. A chambermaid in a Lugano hotel had identified him from the newspaper photograph and notified the police.

Now Simon determined to make full use of the press. He telephoned the United Press in Zurich, Switzerland, and asked them to notify the Swiss police, which they did. The

police quickly found Raja and told him he was an un-
desirable alien in their country and he had to leave the
country immediately, but not by airplane. No visa would
be granted him to leave for far-off places. No, he must get
into his little red Fiat and drive to some bordering country.

Simon Wiesenthal dislikes any description of himself as
a manhunter, but a manhunt was just what now developed.
Raja found himself driving hither and thither, with the net
drawing closer and closer around him, with every move he
made reported by newspapers and police.

He tried to get into France, into Germany, and back into
Italy. At each border he was refused admission. Like a
cornered rat he drove frantically from one border to another.
The Swiss police stayed right with him. He was not even
allowed into a hotel to stay overnight. He must have been
savage with frustration. A fortune was in his wallet but
there was no one he could bribe.

Finally, there was only one place he could go because he
was a citizen of that country—Austria. A false tip was leaked
to the newspapers that he would fly there. Crowds of TV
and newspaper reporters and cameramen were waiting for
him at the Viennese airport. He did not arrive.

He was still tricky. He got permission to cross the small
southern strip of Germany by car into Austria and he got
through the Austrian customs unnoticed. Then he drove
without calling any attention to himself across the country
into Vienna, parked his car, and walked into the Justice
building to find a judge who had been an old friend and
surrendered to him. A cooperative judge could find all sorts
of ways to spend so much time on preliminaries that the
excitement would die down; the warrant would get lost;
the trial be put off and off until no one cared any more.

At the same time Simon was in the office of the attorney
general, just returned from his vacation. Raja had to be

put under arrest immediately, Simon was now demanding. "Patience, Herr Wiesenthal. Patience," the attorney general was replying. "I cannot tell you yes or no. I must examine the material against this man Raja. There must be a preliminary inquiry first before any arrest."

During such an inquiry Raja would not be detained. He would be a free man. Who could tell what he might do, where he might escape to, with the power of ODESSA behind him and with the help of influential Viennese?

The anger in Simon built up to a fierce determination. He informed the attorney general that the Jewish Passover had just begun. This was the time to say prayers for the Jewish dead. He had his prayer book in his hand because he had planned to go from the attorney-general's office to the synagogue.

Now he stood up and faced the attorney general across his desk. "Instead of going to the synagogue, I shall stay right here and say the prayers for all the 110,000 Jews of Holland that were sent to concentration camps by Raja-kowitsch."

He meant what he said. He began the chants.

The attorney general was scandalized. Yet what could he do? He couldn't stop the man from praying. If he telephoned the guards to come and carry Wiesenthal out by force, it would become a newspaper sensation. On the other hand, if Wiesenthal stayed there, saying prayers that would go on and on and on for more than one hundred thousand people, the story would be certain to leak out—and the newspapers would be crowding into the office to watch the famous Simon Wiesenthal praying for the souls of all the dead Dutch Jews Rajakowitsch had deported.

He pleaded with Simon to go.

"Very well," Simon answered, "I will go—direct to the newspapers." He would tell them exactly how the attorney general was delaying making an arrest, giving Raja a chance to escape. He reminded the attorney general that all the nations were watching him, and that Holland would be outraged if Eichmann's deputy should escape justice. He would not mention to the newspapers that he was prepared to maintain a prayer vigil in or outside this office—if the arrest was made.

The next morning Simon returned to find his threats had worked. Rajakowitsch was being interrogated at that very moment in the courtroom. Outside that courtroom Simon Wiesenthal watched as Rajakowitsch came out, and two police officers stepped forward to arrest him.

The trial took place in April of 1965. Rajakowitsch was sentenced to only two and one-half years in prison.

Even that was a victory—considering the fact that the Austrian courts were reluctant to sentence any SS man to any stay in any prison. At least, those two years and a half could be considered a kind of Kaddish, the Jewish prayer for the dead.

Chapter Nine

In the case of the Mauer brothers, Johann and Wilhelm Mauer, the peculiar attitude of Austrian justice toward SS criminals almost triumphed again. This time, however, the atmosphere was changing and they did not suffer just a slap on the wrist.

The crimes of the two brothers had been committed in the town of Stanislau, in the province of Galicia in Poland. The few Jews and Poles and Ukranians who survived the Stanislau massacre told this ghastly story:

On October 12, 1941, the Jewish ghetto was surrounded by SS men under the supervision of Johann and Wilhelm Mauer. All the twenty thousand Jewish inhabitants were driven out at gunpoint to the Jewish cemetery. There they were forced to strip naked, hand over all their money, their jewerly and their clothing.

Two large ditches had already been dug. In batches, the Jews were herded up to the edges of these ditches and met by submachine gunfire. As that batch fell into the grave ditch, another was driven up to take their place and, as they died, they fell on top of the first ones. Not all in the grave died immediately. Some, only wounded, were smothered to death by the weight of those falling on them.

The massacre began in the early morning and went on all day long. When darkness came the job was still not finished. Autos and truck were driven up and stationed all around so that their headlights could illuminate the ditches, the victims and their executioners. All through the night the hideous sounds of dying men, women, and children and the crackle of gunfire went on until twenty thousand perished.

The Mauers were hunted after the war but they eluded capture because all of the few survivors in the city of Stanislau gave the brothers name as *Maurer.*

It was only when one investigator was discussing the case with Simon Wiesenthal that Simon suggested there might be one *r* too many in the name. He had had trouble before with witnesses mistaking a name. Besides, the Wiesenthals had lived in that area of Poland, and Simon knew that Mauer was a much more common spelling than Maurer.

Now the brothers were quickly found. Both Johann and Wilhelm were working for a religious, charitable organization in Salzburg, Austria. These two, who had been among the cruelest of SS men, were using religion as a cloak to hide their brutal past.

The Mauers' neighbors and friends and co-workers at the Evangelical Auxiliary Service in Salzburg did not see things that way at all. How could anyone say such terrible things about two such nice, pious, good men! Suppose they did have to kill a few people away off in Poland—it was wartime, wasn't it?

When the trial began it looked as if it would be hard to get a jury. No one wanted to be on it. A jury was finally picked from most reluctant Salzburg citizens. They hardly bothered to listen to the prosecutor or the witnesses. They were only interested in the defense lawyer. The jury handed down its verdict: *Not Guilty.*

This time, however, that verdict was not allowed to stand. The judge ruled it an "obvious error," and ordered a new trial. Before the new trial started the newspapers poured contempt upon the original jury. Young Austrian students paraded the streets of Salzburg carrying placards which read: "AUSTRIA, NATIONAL PARK FOR NAZI CRIMINALS."

Perhaps the older Salzburg citizens were shamed. When the second trial started the new jury was a sober and chastened one. They listened to the witnesses, and Johann Mauer was sentenced to eight years in prison, and his brother Wilhelm was given twelve years.

Austria was waking up. Germany had already established its own head office for the Detection of War Criminals, at Ludwigsburg. Still, Simon Wiesenthal had no illusions that either nation was going to search for and prosecute all the SS men. They had started too late, for one thing. For another, they were not out seeking. If a man were brought to their attention they would act, but there were more prosecutors than investigators.

At a newspaper conference held in Vienna Simon met a man who was bureau chief of the Russian Tass News Agency. The two men talked of many missing SS men, and the Russian mentioned Kurt Wiese. Simon Wiesenthal knew of the crimes of Wiese, but the Russian knew much more since the crimes had taken place in Grodno and in Bialystok in Poland, and Poland was now in the Soviet zone of influence. He told Wiesenthal that the Soviets had collected a big file on Wiese, and he promised to send a copy of all they had to Wiesenthal's Documentation Center.

This was a real favor for governments did not, as a rule, send such material to a private citizen. The reason why the bureau chief shared the file was clear. "I know you're going to use it," the Russian said. "If I give it to the West Germans, they may just bury it in their files."

The material on Wiese was shocking. He was believed to have killed, personally, at least two hundred people. He had shot one man because he had tried to leave the Jewish ghetto without a permit. He had shot a woman who "attempted to take a small piece of bread into the ghetto." He had shot a little girl whose only offense was that "she was playing with a cat." Wiese and other Gestapo men had killed all the forty patients of the Jewish hospital. For no particular reason he had mowed down twenty Jews with his submachine gun, in December 1942. One of the men had only been wounded and he tried to run away; Wiese ran after him and shot him in the head.

The people in the ghetto were starving. They were marched out to work each day, and sometimes a kindly Polish laborer or employer would slip them a piece of bread or meat. Wiese had them searched when they returned and if he found them with any food, he killed them.

In 1963 Simon Wiesenthal heard that Kurt Wiese had been arrested in Cologne, Germany. Immediately he sent all the information the Russian had given him to the proper authorities in Cologne.

They thanked him, but then the courts did something that infuriated him. They allowed Kurt Wiese to go free on bail, pending his trial. Simon wrote them again. He protested vigorously. Allowing Nazi criminals to go free on bail—when they were charged with murder—was just giving them a chance to escape.

There was no answer. In July of 1964, what he had predicted came true. Simon was listening to the evening news broadcast when there came a special announcement: "Kurt Wiese, under indictment for war crimes, has escaped from the apartment in Cologne where he has lived for the past two years. He had been arrested, but was out on bail pending his trial. He'd been ordered to report to the prosecutor's office every third day. When he did not report for a week, detectives went to look for him. They were told by neighbors that Wiese had not been seen for several days. Listeners to this program are asked to report any useful information to the prosecutor's office in Cologne. . . ."

Wiesenthal had a hunch Wiese would come to Austria. He had learned to trust his hunches because they were based on past experience, and on his knowledge of the working of the Nazi fugitive's mind. Under indictment as he was and with his name so prominent in the newspapers, Wiese would hardly have dared to go to any foreign consulate in Cologne to ask for a visa to any country which would not extradite him back to Germany.

No, he would flee to Austria where there was a network of former SS men and sympathizers who would protect him, get a passport for him under a different name and then help him to safety in South America or the Middle Eastern countries.

In spite of what the Milan policemen had thought when Wiesenthal identified Raja, the Documentation Center had no real espionage operation. However, Wiesenthal did have one spy among the old SS "comrades," who was invited to their beer parties and who heard some of their secrets.

The story of this spy, whom Simon Wiesenthal always called Alex (that was not his real name), was a strange and tragic one. He had been a boy in his teens when Hitler came to power. He was the son of a Catholic mother and his father

was a Jewish engineer. Being half-Jewish he would be subject
to the dangers all Jews faced, so his parents gave him to a
Gentile doctor who claimed him as his own.

The boy grew up. He joined the Waffen (the Army) SS,
in the hope that this, somehow, might save his real father
from persecution. It did not. While Alex was with the army
fighting in Russia, his father was taken off to a concentration camp.

Alex knew that his SS group was shooting civilians, not
soldiers, but he honestly believed what he was told: they
were spies and saboteurs and purely coincidence that most of
the victims were Jews. Then Alex himself was wounded and
placed in a hospital room with two other SS men. They soon
enlightened him. They had worked in concentration camps.

He was so revolted by the SS uniform he wore that he
volunteered for the regular army when he got out of hospital,
and was captured, fighting, by the Russians. He had spent
six years in a prison camp before the war ended and he was
sent home.

When he first told his story to Simon Wiesenthal he was
tortured by the fact that he, a Jew, had belonged to the Jew-
killing SS elite corps. He was still accepted by his former SS
comrades, and Simon proposed to Alex that he pretend to
still think and act like one of them, but secretly he would
work for the Documentation Center.

So when Wiesenthal had his hunch Kurt Wiese would
come to Austria, he telephoned Alex and asked him to find
out anything he could. Alex phoned him back the next
evening and spoke in their code. "The goods," he said, was
on its way to the city of Graz in Austria. Alex would visit
that city to look after "the goods."

The next night Alex called again, from Graz. He must
have been calling from a safe place because he spoke more
plainly, and excitedly.

"One of the comrades (the SS Kameraden) here told me that a man who pretends to be a refugee from the Soviet Zone of Germany has just arrived in town. Could it be the fellow we're looking for?"

"Maybe he isn't," answered Wiesenthal. "But it would be somebody else who is interesting."

"One of the comrades put him up for the night. This morning he spent an hour with Herbert Berghe von Trips," said Alex.

Immediately Simon Wiesenthal knew his hunch had been right. "Trips!" he said. "Then it *must* be the man we're looking for."

Trips had been a Gestapo commissar and the last commander of Pawiak Prison in Warsaw. Wiesenthal had tried, for a long time, without success, to get the Austrian Ministry to investigate this man. Trips was powerful, the very sort of man ODESSA might choose to mastermind the escapes of wanted men in Austria.

Alex quickly added that the man who claimed to have escaped from the Soviet Union was a Hubert Zimmermann, who limps heavily with his right leg. "He left Graz about an hour ago. But I know where he . . ."

The phone went dead. Wiesenthal did not worry about that. Alex must have had his own reasons for hanging up so suddenly.

Simon Wiesenthal thought about the name and the description. Kurt Wiese did limp. And a Herbert Zimmermann had been a commander of both Wiese and Trips during the war. Perhaps Zimmermann had given Wiese his passport, or perhaps he had just taken the name. The real Zimmermann was under indictment for war crimes in Germany.

The telephone in the Vienna office rang early the next morning. It was Alex.

"Sorry I couldn't finish my report last night. I spoke from

a hotel in Graz. Just then a comrade came in. Now I am speaking from a public telephone on the highway to Semmering." Semmering was a famous mountain resort about sixty miles south of Vienna. "Hubert Zimmermann is registered at a large hotel at the resort, where he is being taken care of by an old friend named Eberhard Gabriel."

Wiesenthal knew a great deal about Eberhard Gabriel, who had been a former SS man and was now the night receptionist at the hotel.

The next day Alex reported that von Trips had called for Zimmermann and driven him in to Vienna for the day. Wiesenthal immediately got in touch with Dr. Wiesinger of the Ministry of the Interior, to ask if the Germans had asked the Austrian authorities to search for Wiese. No, replied Dr. Wiesinger. What made Simon think Wiese could be here? Simon answered that Wiese *was* here, he was in Semmering and he was tall, fifty years old, wore a dark-gray suit and glasses, and had a limp in his right leg. He urged Dr. Weisinger to get in touch with the police in Cologne and begin the necessary paperwork to arrest and send Wiese back for his trial.

For three days Simon kept after Dr. Wiesinger—who was doing nothing—and listened for phone calls from Alex, who was doing a lot. Alex reported that each day Zimmermann had driven in to Vienna, where he probably was arranging for his escape from Europe. Then on the fourth day, a Tuesday, July 21, Alex called and urged Simon to come to Semmering where they could meet safely at an appointed place.

When Simon arrived Alex was plainly agitated. "We've got to work fast, or Wiese is going to get away forever. He's gone to the Egyptian Embassy in Vienna twice. Apparently he has a stolen passport, but he's had some trouble with the Egyptian officials. They are reluctant to issue him an Egyptian visa in Vienna. Also, they don't want him to take a

plane from Vienna to Cairo. Instead, they suggested that
Wiese take a train to Belgrade and go to the Egyptian Embassy there. There are frequent flights from Belgrade to
Cairo. So that's the setup. Wiese plans to leave for Graz on
the 4:05 A.M. express train from Semmering. From Graz it's
easy to get to Belgrade."

4:05 A.M. And it was now ten o'clock in the evening.
Simon had six hours in which to stop Wiese and he could
only stop him with an official Austrian arrest. Once Wiese
was in Egypt he would be free. Egypt had refused before to
extradite such men.

Alex stayed in Semmering to keep an eye on Wiese, while
Simon Wiesenthal drove back to Vienna and called up Dr.
Wiesinger and explained the circumstances to him.

Dr. Wiesinger explained that he could do nothing until
Germany sent him a description of the missing Wiese to
compare with Wiesenthal's description of Zimmermann.

The next hours were frantic ones. Simon put through a
call to the Federal Criminal Agency in Wiesbaden, Germany,
asking for an exact description of Wiese. The official at
the other end of the phone replied he could not give out
such information to an unauthorized civilian. Then, demanded Simon, to whom would he give it?

"I'll try to get it to the Austrian Interpol. I'm sorry,"
stiffly, "but that's the only way of doing it."

The International Criminal Police Organization, com-
monly known as Interpol, could be most effective. They
were geared to move lightning-fast—but only if that official
really moved to alert them in time.

Simon could not be sure of that. He called Dr. Wiesinger
again and urged him to telephone Cologne. The Minister,
by this time, was as fully worried about the possibility of
Wiese getting away as was Simon, but when he called
Cologne the prosecutor there was not at his office nor at his

home. And it was now three o'clock in the morning. They had only one hour left.

Dr. Wiesinger was apologetic, but frustrated.

"If you don't send your men to Semmering now, it will be too late," Simon exploded. "A man accused of mass murder is going to get away forever."

"I know," said Dr. Wiesinger, "but I can't arrest a man who has a valid German identity card in the name of Zimmermann only because you claim he isn't Zimmermann but Wiese. He has committed no offense against Austrian law. Two of my men are alerted. As soon as word comes from Germany, we'll proceed, if the information tallies with yours."

Simon hung up. He was alone in his office and just now, in the middle of the night, it seemed a very lonely place. He tried not to look at the clock. It. was a sixty-mile drive to Semmering; even if the Minister's two men left right now they might not make it.

The minutes dragged. There was only the one light on Simon's desk. There was the clock and the telephone. There was himself, sitting tensely hunched in his chair.

The telephone rang. Instinctively Simon looked at the clock: it was eighteen minutes past three. He picked up the receiver. Dr. Wiesinger spoke quickly: "Interpol contacted me just after your last call. Your information was correct. The man is Wiese. I've sent my two officers to Semmering. They're driving a police car with a siren, and they have a chance of getting there just in time. I told them to board the train without being noticed. We don't want too much excitement at the Semmering station . . . I'll call you when I have word."

Now there was hope, and there was also despair. It was an endless, tortured hour of waiting. Could the police get there in time? Four o'clock came and went. Four fifteen—four twenty. Simon's hopes had sunk completely when the phone rang at four twenty-five. Dr. Wiesinger, jubilant, reported his men had captured Kurt Wiese.

Now Simon could go home to bed. In the morning Alex came to tell him his part of the story.

He had stayed around the hotel lobby, and then secretly followed Wiese and the hotel man, Gabriel, to the railroad station. "You can imagine how I felt when I saw Wiese shake hands with Gabriel and get on the train. I knew the train was leaving in three minutes. *Three minutes!* At that moment the two detectives arrived. The train was already beginning to move but they managed to get aboard the last coach. I heard a whistle and saw the train disappear into the Semmering tunnel."

Simon questioned the two police detectives that day and heard the rest of the story. They had waited just a little while and then made their way slowly through the coaches. They came to a compartment where a solitary man was sitting with his right leg stretched out. They stood outside in the corridor and watched him. He got up to reach for a newspaper—and he limped.

They stepped inside the compartment. "Herr Wiese," said one of the policeman, very sharply.

It was an old trick of the police, to catch a man off guard, and it worked. The man in the compartment looked up from his newspaper and nodded his head in agreement before he remembered that his name was not supposed to be Wiese. He stuttered, shook his head—"My name is—."

"We know, Herr Wiese. You're traveling under the name of Hubert Zimmermann. Let's see your identification card, please."

The train came to a stop for the next station. Wiese was

in agony as they studied his card. He was so close to the Austrian border, so close to freedom. Then he heard the words:

"You're under arrest, Herr Wiese."

He was brought back to Vienna, where he confessed his identity, and was sent back to Cologne. There would be no bail for him this time while he awaited his trial. The wait might take some time because the German authorities were attempting to fill out their case against him. The information the Soviets had turned over only covered a couple of years and there must be a great deal more that Kurt Wiese had to account for.

Back in Vienna both Simon Wiesenthal and Alex knew they were finished with that case. And it amused them both that the Kameraden were becoming very suspicious of one another, around Graz and Semmering. Who had tipped off the Austrian police?

They never suspected Alex.

Simon Wiesenthal's life was not all made of up grim pursuits and exciting chases. In spite of the ever-present threats from the SS Kameraden that hung over him, his private life was happy. In 1965 his daughter, Pauline, was married. Wiesenthal invited Heinrich Guenthert, his old top boss at the Eastern Railroad Repair Works where Simon and Cyla had both worked as forced labor in Poland, to the wedding.

Guenthert, now an official of the West German Federal Railroads, was overcome at the invitation. It seemed to him remarkable that Simon should remember that he had tried to be decent in his treatment of all the workers, Poles or Jews. "When a man like Simon Wiesenthal, after all that happened, invites a German to join his family, I feel honored," he said.

And he recalled his impression of Simon as a man who stood out among all the others because "he always walked with his head up and looked me straight in the eye. The SS men said Wiesenthal was impertinent. . . . I was impressed by the man's erect bearing."

The Wiesenthals would have invited Adolf Kolhrautz, the Inspector who helped him to escape the Repair Works, but Kolhrautz was dead.

Other people besides Guenthert were impressed by Wiesenthal's "erect bearing" and his way of looking straight in the eye at the person he was talking to, whether that person was friend or foe. Dedicated as he was to his work, and after all he had gone through under the Nazis, no threats, no bullying, no amount of pompous authority displayed by judges or government officials, could frighten him.

At one time he faced Dr. Christian Broda, the Minister of Justice for Austria. Dr. Broda was furious that Wiesenthal was demanding he look into the past history of some of the appointed Austrian judges. Simon asked that Broda clean out those who had been Nazi judges carrying out the worst of Nazi laws. Dr. Broda finally slammed his hand down on his desk and shouted that he would tolerate no more interference by Wiesenthal in his Ministry of Justice.

Simon Wiesenthal remained calm and undisturbed.

"Herr Minister," he said, "you cannot shout at me. I'm not here on behalf of a wealthy client who pays me a lot of money to represent his interests. And I was not appointed as the lawyer for six million dead people. But I've worked for over twenty years for the memory of these people, and I believe I've earned the right to speak for them. Will you deprive me of this right?"

Dr. Broda said nothing for a moment. He tried to meet the dark, compelling eyes fixed on him. He must have been

thinking of Wiesenthal's reputation and his influence with
so many newspapers, so many people. There was danger in
insulting such a man. Reluctantly he said, 'I'll concede this
right to you. But only to you, Herr Wiesenthal."

Dr. Broda was right to fear Wiesenthal's power and influence. Newspapermen flocked to any press conference he
called. He was now constantly being asked to speak at youth
meetings, Catholic and Protestant as well as Jewish. Organizations in Israel and the United States and Holland and
Germany paid Wiesenthal's way so he could be their prominent speaker.

Letters came to him simply addressed *Wiesenthal, Vienna.*
The post office delivered them. One letter was sent to *Simon
Wiesenthal, Manager, The Research Institute for Nazi
Crimes, Munich, Germany.* The Munich post office knew
who he was and where he was; they re-addressed the letter
and it reached Simon.

Bruno Marek, Mayor of Vienna, said to him: 'Herr Wiesenthal, you sometimes make life very difficult for us but we
need you: you are the voice of our conscience vis-à-vis the
Jews."

He *did* make people uncomfortable. When he spoke to
large or small groups he did not try to lighten his remarks
with small jokes. He told them plain truths and hard facts.
Sometimes he grew emotional and then his eyes would flash;
sometimes he used a cutting irony to make a point. He was
no actor, but the depths of his feelings gave him the force
of a great actor on a stage.

"Wiesenthal talks," said one man who had been in his
audience, "and a cold draft seems to go through the room.
I didn't know that such men existed outside of the Old
Testament. He is the watcher and the warner, and he's been
right so often that no one dares ignore him."

He has a mystical sense of his mission. Nothing can make him angrier than the people who say "why bother about all those Nazis now? The war's been over a long time." He remembers one American officer who couldn't understand what all the fuss was about. As he said, "Nazis and anti-Nazis, weren't they just the same as Democrats and Republicans at home? Two different parties, that was all."

Simon Wiesenthal is fighting an idea—the Nazi idea. That idea is carried by men, so he pursues the men. He sees ex-SS men scattered all over the world, many of them rich and influential, still poisoning the minds of men with theories. They teach that some men are born to rule while others are born to be their slaves; that whole groups of people are inferior and unfit to live just because of their race, their religion or their color.

Simon would not be keeping faith with all the millions dead if he did not keep up the pressure on their murderers. He knew now where some of the worst of them were hiding:

Dr. Josef Mengele In Paraguay

Heinrich Muller (Chief of the Gestapo and for years presumed to be dead) Now rumored to be in Argentina

Rolf Guenther (Eichmann's deputy, presumed dead) In Argentina

Alfons Willem Sassen (wanted for mass murder in the Netherlands) Now in Lima, Peru

Klaus Barbie (Gestapo chief in France who deported French Jews to concentration camps) La Paz, Boliva

Gustav Wagner (sub-commandant of Treblinka and Sobibor camps) In Brazil

Dr. Andrida Artukovich (Nazi Croatian Minister of Justice, deported twenty-five thousand Jews to concentration camps) Living in the United States, where his lawyers had successfully defeated an attempt to deport him.

Valerian Trifa United States

Hermine Braunsteiner United States

Chapter Ten

Nazis in the United States? Murderers here? And protected by our laws and citizenship? Yes.

When Simon Wiesenthal was invited to lecture in the United States in 1964, he gave an interview to *The New York Times* in which he claimed that—among other Nazis here—there was a Mrs. Hermine Braunsteiner Ryan, living quietly in Queens, New York, as an ordinary housewife.

Under the name of Hermine Braunsteiner in Germany she had been no ordinary person. She had been the notoriously cruel guard and supervisor at both Ravensbruck and Maidenek concentration camps.

Newspaper men swarmed to Queens to interview Mrs. Ryan. They found it hard to believe that this middle-aged woman, cleaning her house and shopping and cooking just like so many other American women, had once been in charge of over eleven thousand women prisoners at a death camp—and that she had tortured and beaten and killed them.

The West German government believed it. They knew it was true. The German government asked the United States to deport her so she could stand trial for her crimes.

How had she gotten to the United States and how had she been able to become a citizen? Somehow she had been able to escape from Germany and emigrate to Canada. In Canada she had married an American citizen. When they moved to Queens, New York, she had applied for naturalization and had become a citizen in 1963. It seems incredible that the Immigration and Naturalization Service would not have questioned anyone who declared in her application that she had lived in Germany during the years of Hitler, whether or not she had been a Nazi Party member. She was not questioned.

However, there was a statement all applicants for citizenship must sign stating that they had never engaged in acts against a minority because of race, creed or national origin. Mrs. Hermine B. Ryan had signed this statement. Since Jews, in Hitler Germany, were considered a race, and since she also ill-treated Poles and other nationals, she had lied. She most certainly could be denaturalized because of this lie.

The process of deporting a citizen was complicated. First, she had to be denaturalized and her citizenship taken away. The individual could fight this, and Mrs. Ryan did. She hired very expensive lawyers and they began filing motions which would stall any action taken.

Even so, the INS had the power to squash her lawyers' motions, take her into court and proceed against her. The INS did absolutely nothing about the Ryan case for seven long years after the Wiesenthal exposé.

Why? Perhaps it was embarrassment. Perhaps they hoped people would just forget that the INS had granted citizenship to a war criminal. Perhaps it was just that the huge bureaucratic organization of the INS was slow-moving. It might have been caution. The Supreme Court had ruled in another case that there must be "clear, unequivocal, and convincing evidence" against someone to take away citizenship. In Mrs. Ryan's case most of her victims were dead, and the survivors might not be available as witnesses.

All these were not really reasons; they were excuses. Simon Wiesenthal—and several people inside the INS—strongly suspected that influential people and a great deal of money was being used to stall the case inside the INS, with the eventual design of dropping it entirely.

All these guesses and questions came to a head when the Assistant Commissioner for Investigations, INS, came to Vincent Schiano, INS's chief trial lawyer, and suggested to him that the case be dropped against Mrs. Ryan. Schiano was outraged.

He most certainly would not drop it. On his own he began gathering evidence and witnesses against her. In 1972 he urged that a special investigator be appointed to help him, and Tony de Vito was assigned to the case.

Nothing could have pleased Tony deVito more. While he was with the U.S. Army in World War II he had seen the concentration camp at Dachau when it was first liberated. He had never forgotten the nauseating horror of the piles of human bones, some with flesh still clinging to them. He could never forget the barely living skeletons, the ones who could totter towards him and the ones too weak to get off their board bunks.

If Hermine Braunsteiner Ryan had been guilty of treating human beings in this fashion, Tony deVito was determined she should not be an American citizen. She should be deported to stand trial for her crimes.

DeVito had not then heard of ODESSA, but he was soon aware that some powerful forces were working against his investigation. The witnesses he brought from Europe were threatened by mysterious phone calls. The callers warned "all Jews will be killed" and "Jew witnesses will die." DeVito's own wife was telephoned by someone who would not give his name but demanded she get her husband off the case.

Then came a day when deVito finished questioning twelve witnesses from the Maidenek concentration camp. He had taken copious notes. On the top of a legal-size note pad he had written each witness's name, address, and phone number in the United States, and then each story. After it was all over he had made a folder for each witness and placed all of the folders in the bottom of a filing cabinet which was then locked with a combination lock.

Only he and Schiano and the security officer on duty on that floor of the INS office building knew the combination of that lock. Yet the next morning, seven of the twelve folders with all their notes were missing.

He and Schiano raised a rumpus and an investigation into the missing files was started. It started—and stopped. Nothing was ever discovered. The missing folders were never found.

DeVito had more than just a suspicion that people *inside* the INS were working against him and for Mrs. Ryan. He had no proof against anyone. He could not press charges against anyone, but it was all linked in his mind with the huge amounts of money that were being spent to hire the Barry law firm (which specialized in immigration work) and to pay the expenses of the Barry lawyers' two trips to Europe to find witnesses for Mrs. Ryan's defense. Her husband was an electrical construction worker, and there was no way he could afford such expense.

DeVito was reading everything he could get his hands on about Hitler's Germany. He read about Simon Wiesenthal and his work. The next day he spoke to Vincent Schiano and said: "I now realize what we're up against, Vince. I'm sure of it. Vince, have you ever heard of an organization called ODESSA?"

Against all odds the two men forged ahead with their

preparations and finally, late in 1972, Mrs. Ryan was brought to trial. The witnesses' testimony was devastating, nor could the witnesses be shaken under the defense lawyers' cross-examination.

One woman testified that she saw Mrs. Ryan whip a concentration camp prisoner to death.

Another told how Mrs. Ryan had ordered a little fourteen-year-old girl hung because the girl had tried to claim she was not Jewish in order to escape the gas chamber. Mrs. Ryan not only ordered the hanging, she forced the other prisoners to watch. The girl was too small; the rope would not reach her neck. Mrs. Ryan commanded a guard to fetch a stool for her to stand on. Before the stool was kicked away the little girl faced the other prisoners and said: "Remember me!"

DeVito felt that no one in that courtroom, listening to this story, could ever forget that girl—or what Hermine Ryan had done.

In the face of such testimony, Mrs. Ryan voluntarily gave up her U. S. citizenship and was extradicted to West Germany in May, 1973. She went on trial with twelve other former guards in November, 1975, in Düsseldorf. As of the writing of this book, the trial had not yet reached its end.

Now Wiesenthal came on another lecture tour and announced that there were more than seventy prominent Nazis still living free in America.

Most of these were not German, and that was the difficulty. People tended to think of Nazis as only German and, perhaps, Austrian. In almost every European country there had been men working secretly or openly for Hitler or Hitler's ideas. Some countries even had large organizations of these people. It did not matter what they called themselves—Utashi or Iron Guard—they were Nazis.

When Germany conquered their countries, or drew them into its sphere voluntarily, these home-grown Nazis were rewarded with high positions. At the end of the war, since they did not have German names and the Allies were not aware of their activities, it was easy for them to escape. If they were found when the Soviets overran those eastern countries, they were given short trials and little mercy.

If they escaped, however, they had excellent chances of passing themselves off as refugees from the communism that was now dominating their countries. So little was known in the United States about Yugoslavia and Rumania and Hungary that no one in the INS seriously questioned the stories of men with such odd names as Trifa and Soobsokov. Instead, they were met here with great sympathy because of the strong anti-Communist feeling during the late 1940's and 1950's.

America *should* learn about these men. Vigorously Simon Wiesenthal wrote and lectured about them, especially about such men as Trifa. Nor was Wiesenthal the only one: a New York dentist, Dr. Charles Kremer, was obsessed by Trifa. Kremer hammered away at INS, at members of congress, the President, and the newspapers about Trifa.

Perhaps some of Kremer's letters went unread. Perhaps not everyone in the government read Simon's newspaper interviews. But surely some people in the government knew the truth. They may have hesitated to do anything because Valerian Trifa, refugee, was now Bishop Valerian Trifa of the Rumanian Orthodox Church diocese in northern Michigan. Bishops seem awesome people, too holy to touch.

Bishop Trifa had friends in high places. On May 11, 1955, Vice-President Nixon invited him to offer the prayer at the opening of the Senate. The short, stocky clergyman, wearing black horn-rimmed glasses, bowed his head and intoned:

"Almighty God . . . who has made America trustee of

priceless human liberty and dignity, look down from Heaven upon Thy servants now present before Thee, and bless them, that they may remember in their discussions and decisions Rumania and all oppressed nations who are still longing for a 'government by the people, and for the people. . . ."

When Simon Wiesenthal read of this he wondered that God had not struck the man dead on the spot.

First of all, Trifa was a fake clergyman. He had never been ordained a priest. He had gotten the title of Bishop by trickery and brutal force.

Secondly, and most important, Trifa had been a leading member of the Iron Guard in Rumania, which had ruled the Rumanian people at gunpoint before and after the Germans had taken over the country. Every act of Trifa had been against liberty, against any government by and for the people of Rumania. It was Trifa who had personally led his youth squads in a mad three-day rampage of beating and killing Jews, burning Jewish homes and businesses and synagogues. This was the man who could piously pray before the United States Senate for the "oppressed nations" and speak of "priceless human liberty and dignity"?

Viorel (or Valerian) Trifa had been a student in a theological seminary when he joined the Iron Guard. He quickly rose to become a commandant, and later was one of its three top leaders. The Iron Guard was determined upon a Nazi Rumania, and in 1940 forced King Carol to abdicate. His son, Michael, became a puppet king in the hands of the Iron Guard. General Antonescu was the real ruler of the country. Immediately one hundred and twenty thousand German Nazi troops entered Rumania, with no opposition, and by November of 1940 Rumania was a co-partner of the Axis (the countries which fought against the Allies), along with Germany and Italy.

Trifa's official position was President of the Union of Christian Students, which placed him in charge of all Nazi youth work. On November 26 he led a bloody pogrom against the Jews in the city of Ploesti.

He grew impatient with General Antonescu. The General, he felt, was moving much too slowly in Nazifying the country, and especially in carrying out the program of exterminating the Jews. On the evening of January 20, 1941, Trifa led a revolt against Antonescu.

The revolt failed. Antonescu's forces around the palace were too strong. So Trifa turned his revolt into a massacre of the Jews. He had whipped up his young Iron Guardists into wild action; if they could not succeed in storming the palace they could loose all that energy against the Jewish quarters of Bucharest. They went on an orgy of murder and destruction. Placards were distributed—*signed* by Trifa—to be distributed all over the city to encourage others to join them in the massacre.

In part, the placard read: "We demand the replacing of all Masonic and kike sympathizers in government. . . ."

And Trifa made a speech to his seething crowd of six thousand followers, saying:

"People were never equal! . . . These ideas of equality served the kikes. . . . The leadership of the people has fallen into the hands of a group of kikes and Jew lovers who are ruling everything. . . . Even if Adolf Hitler had done nothing else but wage this huge struggle of National Socialism, which leads to the unmasking of the fight against Judaism, he would still have risen to great peaks of history as he blazed a new path."

And then he and the crowd began their hideous massacre.

A report reached the United Rumanian Jews of America in that same year. It gave an eye-witness account of some of the terrors of the night Trifa had inspired:

"Perhaps the most horrifying single episode," the report read, "of the pogrom was the 'kosher butchering' of more than two hundred Jews in the municipal slaughterhouse. There the Greenshirts (as Trifa's young Iron Guardists were called) forced them to undress and led them to the chopping blocks, where they cut their throats in a horrible parody of the traditional Jewish methods of slaughtering fowl and livestock. . . . (The) naked, headless bodies were hung on hooks and stamped 'kosher meat'. . . . The general staff which ordered this massacre consisted of Horia Sima, Dimity Groza . . . and Viorel Trifa. . . ."

In Bucharest alone it was estimated that between four thousand and six thousand Jews died that night, and the massacre was carried out in other parts of Rumania as well. No one knows the real number of the Jewish victims.

Trifa was a hero to his young Greenshirts, but General Antonescu was after his blood. They were both Nazis, but Trifa had dared to revolt against him. A squad was sent to arrest Trifa, but he and the other two leaders of the revolt hid safely until they could escape to Germany. There they found refuge.

The Germans had to work with Antonescu, but they liked Trifa's bolder methods. They wished his revolt had succeeded. They hid him in the German Embassy and then helped smuggle him into Germany and to the camp at Buchenwald.

On his arrival in the United States Trifa claimed he, as an anti-Nazi and anti-Communist fighter, had been in the notorious Buchenwald concentration camp. He lied. His "camp" was attached to Buchenwald but it was called Fichtenheim and was made up of plush, fancy living quarters for people like Trifa whom Germany wanted to protect and use.

Simon Wiesenthal wrote of Fichtenheim: ". . . (they)

could have radios, exercise as many hours as they wanted, or they could work for pay. Food and medical care were the same as for German soldiers. Married men were allowed to live with their wives. . . ."

Trifa worked for the Germans. He made regular radio broadcasts from Germany into Rumania, extolling the wonders of Hitler and urging young Rumanians to enlist to fight alongside the Germans.

At the end of the war Trifa ran to Italy, and there he boldly declared to the occupation American army officers that he had been a victim of the Nazis and interned at Buchenwald. They believed him. He also declared himself a student who had been studying for the priesthood when the Nazis imprisoned him. Catholic clergymen believed him.

For four years he laid low in Italy, teaching history at a Catholic university—but *not* becoming a priest. Then a contact of his in the United States, a priest who had studied with Trifa as a young man in Rumania, agreed to sign the necessary papers for Trifa's admittance to the U.S. as a "displaced person."

When he entered this country he was questioned by Immigration authorities. "Were you ever a member of the Iron Guard?"

"No," said Trifa. And all the rest of his answers were either completely false or half-truths.

He settled in Cleveland, and gradually brought over to this country a whole group of his former Greenshirt Iron Guardists. It was with them that he planned and executed the terrorist takeover of the Rumanian Bishop's position, house, estate, and funds in Michigan.

The planning took years. During that time frequent requests to investigate Trifa were made by Rumanian Jews alerted by Wiesenthal and letters from the dentist, Kremer, to the Immigration and Naturalization Service. He was exposed over and over. The INS ignored the information. As far as they were concerned Trifa was a legitimate refugee and a good anti-Communist.

Trifa was alert to everything that happened inside the Rumanian-American community, and at last he saw his chance. When it became time for the priest Moldovan to become the Bishop, Moldovan had done what all had done before him. He had gone back to Rumania so that his superiors in the Rumanian Orthodox Church could consecrate him and make him a bishop. Then he had returned to Michigan to take up his new office.

Trifa and his men went to every Rumanian in the diocese and told them that what Bishop Moldovan had done was not only illegal but evil. He had gone to a Communist country. Maybe the Rumanian clergymen were now Communists, too. It was, so Trifa declared, an unholy consecration.

The Rumanians were confused and afraid. They certainly did not want a Communist bishop. They were ashamed that their homeland was now a Communist country, so they were anxious to show their fellow Americans that they were more anti-Communist than anyone else. They were persuaded by Trifa that something should be done about Bishop Moldovan.

Of course Trifa's charge was ridiculous. The Orthodox Church inside Rumania operated legally with no pressure upon it to adopt socialist ideas. Only there could a bishop be properly consecrated.

Now Trifa persuaded a Ukranian Bishop of the Ukranian Orthodox Church in America to consecrate him. He claimed this would be legal since the Ukranians and Rumanians

were both part of the same Orthodox Church. He must
have lied again, since only an ordained priest could become
a bishop. Nevertheless, he was now Bishop Valerian Trifa.
He demanded Bishop Moldovan vacate his title and the
Michigan diocese. Naturally, Moldovan refused. Trifa
wasted no more words on him. He had his own gang of
bullies and managed to gather a large crowd of the Rumanians in the district and one day Trifa led nearly a
hundred people to the bishop's estate at Grass Lakes.

Yelling "Communists!" they made an attack on the big
house of twenty-five rooms in which lived Moldovan and
his monks. They threw rocks to break the windows. They
shouted insults. They demanded that Bishop Moldavan
and the monks come out and leave, or they would come in
and drag them out.

Trifa's special squad had already cut the telephone lines.
It was an isolated spot. The police did not come. Whether
the police had been told this was purely a dispute between
Rumanians, and they were not to meddle in this church
business, no one can tell for certain. They had heard it was
a problem between good Rumanian—Americans and some
Communist Rumanians. Whatever the reason, the police
did not interfere.

Like the trained soldiers that they were, Trifa's men surrounded the house, hurling rocks and battering the doors
with thick logs.

Bishop Moldovan was a mild and gentle man; the monks
had never encountered violence in their sheltered, religious
life. Within a short time they came out and surrendered.
The Bishop led his monks through the jeering crowd, and
Valerian Trifa marched in and took over in triumph. He
then consecrated his own men—few of whom had had any
religious training at all—as his monks.

Trifa now had the great, fine house, the two hundred acres, and the church revenues now coming in from the Michigan parishioners. The stories about the takeover were, of course, dictated by Trifa. Bishop Moldovan's protests were ignored. Neither the police, the law courts or the newspapers wanted to meddle into something that seemed to be purely a church matter. All they could understand was that the anti-Communists among the Rumanian-Americans had won out over a bunch of Communists.

Bishop Valerian Trifa emerged as a champion of the American way of life, and was honored for it by then Vice-president Nixon and invited to give the opening prayer to the United States Senate!

But Trifa was not as safe as he thought. Men like Simon Wiesenthal and Charles Kremer, the dentist, never let up on their campaign to expose him, each in his own way. It was not only Trifa's past that worried them; it was his present activities.

Trifa was busy spreading a network of Iron Guardists cells throughout the United States and in Spain and in South America, wherever there were ex-Rumanians. He was issuing a newspaper *Drum* which was filled with hatred and slander against Jews. Trifa was working for the day when America could be incited to war against Rumania, and he could again emerge as a military leader and dictator.

Although again and again the INS turned down Kremer's requests for an investigation, the newspapers were beginning to catch the smell of scandal and rottenness and corruption that hung about Trifa and his gang. They wrote stories that did him no credit. Editorials appeared in magazines and newspapers demanding to know why a former Iron Guard leader had been given citizenship in this country, and why wasn't the INS investigating him now?

The publicity grew to the point where finally something had to be done. On May 16, 1975, the U.S. Attorney in Detroit, Michigan, filed a complaint and began proceedings "to revoke and set aside the order of the court admitting Bishop Trifa to citizenship and to cancel his certificate of naturalization on the grounds that the order was illegally procured . . . by misrepresentation."

To date Trifa's denaturalization hearings have not been concluded. If and when his citizenship is revoked, Trifa can be deported to stand trial in Rumania for his crimes.

This may take many years. His lawyers are fighting every inch of the way, and the case is dragging on year after year. Trifa has money and important friends. He may possibly win and stay here a citizen—to the shame of America.

But not all the ex-Nazis win. On May 31, 1978, Simon Wiesenthal was heartened to hear that a federal judge in Chicago had revoked the citizenship of a Nazi war criminal, Frank Walus, accused of killing some twenty-five to thirty Jews in Poland. Walus will be deported back to Germany to stand trial.

Simon Wiesenthal was also instrumental in the most recent unmasking of a war criminal. It happened in Brazil, of all places the one where Nazis had felt themselves safe from arrest and deportation.

Gustav Wagner had always been on Simon Wiesenthal's list of Most Wanted men. He had been the brutal sub-commandant of both the Treblinka and Sobibor death camps in Poland. Simon Wiesenthal had traced Wagner to Italy and then to Syria, where he had stayed for several years. Then, in 1950, he obtained a visa from the Brazilian Embassy in Syria and had emigrated to Brazil, where he found others just like himself.

They lived well. They felt secure, so secure that they

even dared to hold a Nazi meeting on April 23, 1978, to honor Adolf Hitler's birthday. The meeting was in the house and grounds near the city of Rio de Janeiro.

Word of the projected meeting had gotten around and one man, an anti-Nazi, heard of it. He managed to get close enough, secretly, to the grounds of the house and took a group picture of the men who were celebrating there.

Then he rushed the photograph to Simon Wiesenthal in Vienna.

Simon studied the faces. Naturally, all the men were thirty or more years older than any pictures he had of his wanted men. They had changed in many ways. Tall men might now be stooped; some had become bald; others would be fatter or thinner, or have mustaches or beards. And not all the faces in the photograph were clear. Some were half-turned away from the camera's lens.

But one was full face, and despite the thirty years' differences, Simon Wiesenthal knew him instantly. No matter what that man said his name was now, he had been and was Gustav Wagner. He was the man who had ordered the deaths of hundreds of thousands of people at Treblinka and at Sobibor.

So great had Simon Wiesenthal's fame grown all over the world that the Brazilian police took his word for the identification, and they staked out the house where Wagner lived.

The state of Israel formally asked Brazil to detain Wagner. Austria, Poland, and Germany notified Brazil that they were preparing requests for Wagner's extradition.

Perhaps the South American countries were becoming embarrassed by their reputation for sheltering Nazis, or perhaps Brazil was impressed by the requests from so many other sovereign nations. Whatever the reason Gustav Wagner was arrested in May of 1978 and held in jail while the Brazilian government decided to which country he should be deported.

To Simon Wiesenthal it does not matter which one gets Wagner. Poland, Germany, Austria and Israel all have so much documented information on the man, they will certainly cooperate in his trial. And the material in Wiesenthal's Documentation Center on Wagner will be available to the prosecutor.

Simon Wiesenthal has attended so many trials. He has been called upon as an expert witness in so many cases. Yet, today, he is less interested in bringing a particular individual to justice than he is in speaking and lecturing to people about the lessons to be learned from the past. Nazism must never arise again. The terrible tragedies must never occur again.

He particularly likes to talk to young people. He does not resent their hot give-and-take of debate. When they argue that Hitler must have done some good things in reviving Germany's economy, he is patient with them. He knows the facts. Prosperity under Hitler was a blown-up, hollow thing. Hitler plunged the country into war, and the German people suffered both physically and financially. An economy based on slave labor was never stable.

He is embarrassed at the way some young people regard him: as a romantic figure, a crusading Sherlock Holmes, a St. George attacking evil with the sword of truth. If occasionally there has been a flash of brilliant deduction, he knows that most of his work and time has been spent in the plodding accumulation of facts and then the tiresome job of fitting one fact to another as if putting together a jigsaw puzzle.

He laughs at the idea that he is any shining knight in armor. His hair is gray and balding, his waist is thickening, his once straight shoulders are beginning to stoop. Yet the old fire and energy are still there and the sword of purpose is still clean and shining. Perhaps the young people who look upon him with awe and gratitude and a romantic idolization may be closer to the real estimation of the character of Simon Wiesenthal than he knows.

BIBLIOGRAPHY

Blum, Howard. *Wanted: The Search for Nazis in America.* New York: Quadrangle, 1976.

Forsyth, Frederick. *The Odessa File.* New York: Viking, 1972.

Frank, Anne. *The Diary of a Young Girl.* New York: Pocket Books, 1972.

Gilbert, G. M. *Nuremberg Diary.* New York: New American Library, 1961.

Heydecker, Joseph J. and Leeb, Johannes. *The Nuremberg Trial.* Cleveland: World, 1962.

Phillips, Peter. *The Tragedy of Nazi Germany.* New York: Praeger, 1969.

"Simon Wiesenthal," *Current Biography*, 1975.

Wiesenthal, Simon. *The Murderers Among Us.* New York: McGraw-Hill, 1967.

Index

ABOUT THE AUTHOR

Writing and traveling fascinate Iris Noble. "In what other profession," she says, "could I carry my office with me? Typewriter in hand, suitcase stuffed with reams of paper, I can be off to work and yet at the same time visit all the exciting places in the world."

She was born in Calgary, Canada, of American parents, and during her early years lived on a ranch in the Crow's Nest Pass. When she was eleven, she moved with her family to Oregon where she attended elementary school in Portland and graduated from Oregon City High School. She majored in English at the University of Oregon and did graduate work at Stanford University in California. She worked as a secretary and as a publicity-advertising director before her marriage to author Hollister Noble in 1941. When they moved soon afterward to New York City, Mrs. Noble began writing magazine articles and gradually moved into books. She has been writing exclusively for young people—biography and fiction—ever since. The urge to travel has sent her throughout Europe, Asia and Africa, researching for new biographical subjects.